SOCIAL DEVIANCE

SOCIAL DEVIANCE

S. Giora Shoham

TEL AVIV UNIVERSITY

Gardner Press Inc., New York
Distributed by Halsted Press Division
John Wiley & Sons, Inc.
New York • Toronto • London • Sydney

GARDNER PRESS, Inc.
32 Washington Square West
New York 10011

Distributed solely by the HALSTED PRESS Division
of John Wiley & Sons, Inc., New York

Library of Congress Cataloging in Publication Data

Shoham, Shlomo.
    Social deviance.

    Bibliography: p.
    Includes index.
    1. Deviant behavior. I. Title.
HM291.S533   301.6'2   76-4788
ISBN 0-470-15076-9 (Halsted)

Printed in the United States of America

1 2 3 4 5 6 7 8 9

In memory of my son
GIORA SHOHAM
Who died in Egypt in the War of the Day of Atonement

Contents

Acknowledgments

The author wishes to express his thanks and appreciation to the Director and Staff of the United Nations Social Defense Research Institute in Rome for making possible a whole summer of theoretical meanderings.

The practical important work of the institute might not directly profit from theories on social deviance, although it could be relevant to it in the wider context of social problems. Kurt Lewin has already aptly stated that there is nothing so practical as a good theory.

Foreword

Since the birth of social science, and surely for many centuries before—in fact since the very first myths that were for so long literally interpreted—humanity has been interested in understanding and fascinated by watching the transgressor, the violator of the normative demands that are made upon all of us. In the Garden of Eden, Eve was tempted and she disobeyed; and the Lord exercised what any modern sociologist would call social control through punitive sanctions. In the next generation, there was fratricide, the first great symbolic expression of man's inhumanity to man, and a warning that brotherhood would remain a universal chimera. Philosophers turned their attention to the deviant; so did physicians, social scientists, and particularly, with remarkable insights, the great men of letters. Where can we learn more about murder, incest, suicide, and betrayal, about violence, cruelty, greed, lust, and, yes, alienation, than from Sophocles, Shakespeare, Goethe, Dostoyevsky, Hugo, down to our own contemporaries, Faulkner and Genet? And nevertheless, what do we know today that was not known, or at least suspected, decades and centuries ago? Is there a murderer in these last decades of the twentieth century, whose mind, psyche, and motivations have been analyzed and studied in interviews and question-naires, who can be understood any more clearly than Dostoyevsky understood Raskolnikov?

Deviance is of the deepest concern to us—not the insignificant differences that distinguish one individual from almost all others in his group, but deviance that violates a norm of a social order (assuming that there is order in society, and assuming that there is such a thing as society, so that putting the two together we come out with social order). We are all of us frightened, yet sometimes envious of the freedom of those who are not as restrained as we are. We admire the creativity that we see in some of the deviants. Although we know that most of us are uncreative, slavish followers, rather than innovators, at the same time, we are hopeful that the creative forces within the artist, philosopher, and political rebel be unleashed without the concomitant victimization of self and others that deviance so often brings with it.

We have learned much from the studies, analyses, demographic research, observations, and autobiographies, that constitute the literature on crime and deviance. This literature has a staggering volume, but it has not yet led to acceptable social policy. Perhaps the time has come to set aside momentarily, our computerized programs, our funded research, our correlations between two variables while we hold a third one constant, and take stock of what we have, synthesize what can be brought together, discard what has been disproved or is of little use, and search for new breakthroughs, not of facts, but of understanding. Any such program will require scholarship in areas new to most social scientists, yet without in any way ignoring or downplaying the very real contributions made by sociology and its related fields. It means gathering threads from theology and mythology, from history and law, from such diverse figures as Hobbes, Rousseau, Marx, Durkheim, Simmel, and Freud and interweaving them with the paradigms, models, research findings, speculations, theories, and analyses of Sellin, Merton, and Sutherland. We need to develop more than a summary; we need a powerful and penetrating approach focused sharply on an important and ofttimes tragic element of the human condition. That is what one finds in this book; and in my view and to my knowledge, nowhere else can it be found with such an economy of words and such an abundance of insights.

Perhaps it is one of the touchstones by which we judge the value of a work of ideas that we can take issue with it as we admire it, and that we find that our disagreements do not lead us to denigrate the work but, on the contrary, to see it as all the more admirable. I do not share Shoham's dismissal of the new biology and its input into understanding human behavior, and I am less than enamored by his fascination for the language and typologies of Freud. At times he is Freudian, which left me sceptical, and at other times he seems to be anti psychiatry, embracing Szasz and Laing. Yet he is not exactly either, for he always offers his own interpretations and reservations, as befits a creative mind. For Shoham is able to bring seemingly contradictory and disparate approaches together, and the whole he creates is much greater than the sum of the many parts he has used.

In the end, Shoham leads us to a point not entirely original, which is that deviance is a form of, an expression of, not merely a result of, social conflict. The antithesis of conflict, in this system, is stagnation, but to leave it at that point is misleading, on the one hand, and irresponsibly dangerous, on the other. Stagnation is always undesirable, whether in individual, group, or society, but change is not always desirable, and can hardly be equated with progress. One can pray, with pious optimism, that through upheaval change will ultimately lead to truth and to human amelioration; but prayer belongs in the house of theology and not in the house of science, and optimism, if one may interpret Shoham and not merely read him, is hardly a part of his world outlook. It is not a happy thought to accept the concept of salvation through pollution, and yet this is what Shoham presents to us, in a seductively way—

although one may hope that his argument is not unassailable.

For this study ends just there: salvation through pollution. Creativity through deviance, chance through the efforts and activities of not only those who shake their fists at humanity (to use a phrase from that much honored creative deviant, Andre Gide), but those whose violations are violent, are depredations, are threats to the survival of you and of me, of Shoham and of the peaceful individual walking on a college campus or a city street. Shoham leaves his argument there. Like almost all important works in social philosophy, this book does not have the answers; it illuminates the scene by posing the proper questions. With his conflict, rather than equilibrium, model of society he takes the reader to a new horizon. But although this book helps us to see further, the sight is gloomy and the tasks are formidable. If deviance brings in its wake social change, and hopefully progress (for change and its direction can be controlled), are there no alternate roads for the achievement of such change, that do not entail so much personal suffering and tragic upheaval? How much violence and nonconformity, normlessness and alienation, unpredictable idiosyncratic activities that are directed against the social body and its individual members can a society tolerate without falling into decline? Or, more likely, without creating a power gap that will be filled by the most repressive and authoritarian groups within that society?

And is the flicker of light from a candle worth it

when it causes our house to burn down? Could Raskolnikov not have been saved without axing the pawnbroker and her sister? Could American society not have learned the meaning of violence without My Lai and the Manson murders; and in fact, after both, is there not reason to suspect that lessons were learned only by those who knew them before? Did Genet have to be a thief, to have suffered and to have brought the suffering on others, in order to fulfill his creative genius? And if he had to be, was his contribution to mankind worth the tragedies wrought upon himself and others?

No other work on deviance, on crime or nonconformity, on creativity or social change, has brought me to confront these questions as inescapably as Shoham has. After reading his book, your head may not rest easier on the pillow; but do you want it to, in these days of turbulence, in these critical years? Actually, Shoham is playing the role of (or actually being) the deviant here; like the deviant, he is taking us all by the neck and shaking us, forcing us to look at things we have been avoiding, challenging us to think through the problems that are within and around us. Hopefully, most of his readers, and therefore social science and society, will benefit by what is at one and the same time a necessary, an unpleasant, and a remarkable experience.

And indeed, that is the message and the task of deviance, as Shoham describes it, in a work that is a brilliant creative achievement.

EDWARD SAGARIN
PROFESSOR OF SOCIOLOGY
CITY COLLEGE OF NEW YORK
JANUARY 1976

Everything which is a source
of solidarity is moral, everything
which forces man to take account
of other men is moral . . . and morality
is as solid as these ties are numerous
and strong. We can see how inexact it
is to define it, as is often done,
through liberty. It rather consists
in a state of dependence.

EMILE DURKHEIM
The Division of Labor in Society

So this is hell. I'd never have believed
it if you remember all we were told about
the torture chambers, the fire and brimstone,
old wive's tales. There is no need
for red-hot pokers. Hell is other people.

JEAN-PAUL SARTRE
No Exit

CHAPTER *I*

INTRODUCTION

Some Basic Premises

*T*he decision as to who is a deviant and who is not is inevitably anchored in a value judgment. Although value judgment is one of the recognized anathemas of social science, the possibility of a value-free sociology has been doubted even by sociologists(1). There are, of course, some social phenonema that may be studied with a certain degree of rational disinterestedness, although never with the lack of involvement displayed by a mathematician analyzing a quadratic equation; the study of social deviation is not one of them.

Deviation is defined as an aberration, a turning from the right course, an obliquity of conduct. By describing someone as deviant, therefore, we express an attitude; we morally brand him and stigmatize him with our value judgment. Social deviation, like crime, is considered a social ill or a social problem. We study the causes and pressures leading to crime and deviation in order to devise better ways and means to combat and prevent them. Emile Durkheim, for instance, assumed that "everything which is a source of solidarity is moral, and morality is as solid as those ties are numerous and strong" (2). Durkheim's original conception of deviance was that the unadjusted are by definition detrimental to the interests of the group, and their faulty solidarity invariably injures the group itself. Consequently, one of the vital norms of every group must be that the individuals comprising it should adjust to its normative system and values. "Adjustment" in itself implies the use of power and pressure to chip the corners of a square peg so that it fits into a round hole. Statistically, *adjustment* means not to deviate from the modal value of the normal curve; philosophically, it is related to the Greek idea of *meden agan* (nothing in excess), engraved on the temple of Apollo at Delphi.

Social deviance is the departure of human beings from rules. This is the most we can say at this point without involving ourselves in premature dilemmas. Individuals may conform to the rules of a minority group, for instance a crime syndicate, which is clearly deviant in relation to the normative system of American society as a whole. A member of a group may reject its values, but may still be a conformist as far as his outward behavior is concerned. A Russian citizen, say, who does not believe in Marxism but behaves as if he does for fear of punishment. Or, a person's performance may be within the mean of the group members' achievement, but deviate from the expectations of law givers and norm setters in the group as, for instance, in some religious orders that set high goals of asceticism for their members.

In this book I shall stress the social attributes of deviance, and exclude physical deformities and biological conspicuities, as opposed to the approach of Erving Goffman, who in his study of the labelling of deviants, included cripples, the blind, the deaf, Jews, Negroes, drug addicts, prostitutes, and homosexuals (3). Our concern will be with deviance that relates to social roles and statuses. That is to say, instead of focussing on the fact that Kierkegaard's physical deformity related him to the minority group of hunchbacks, we will be concerned with how his self-concept as a cripple contributed to his bizarre and painful relationships with other people, especially women.

Actually, adjustment is a virtue prescribed by the group whose interest (that is, whose solidarity) it serves. The group has the power to enforce adjustment, and to apply sanctions to those who are maladjusted. The axiomatic value judgment of the Durkheimian tradition is that group cohesion, solidarity, and conformity are "functional," that is, useful to the group; they are social, as opposed to antisocial, and *good*. This point of view excludes the possibility that a society, although cohesive and full to the brim with solidarity, may be antisocial, deviant, and bad. As Nettler remarked, "The possibility

that a society may be 'organized' on antisocial or un-
ethical principles has been voiced by novelists—a possibility which Durkheim would have regarded as a con-
tradiction in terms" (4).

We may however relate Durkheim's reliance on
solidarity to the human quest for security and stability
through social institutions. This quest is apparent in the
importance of the authoritarian but comforting bosom
of the Catholic Church, which swathed mankind in a
cosy cocoon of meaning, and provided an orderly everafter. To be outside the Church meant not only losing
one's soul, but also being an outlaw. For this sense of
belonging and meaningfulness, the individual was expected to repay the group with conformity and
solidarity. This was not too high a price for security and
stability; indeed, most individuals were glad to renounce
a freedom that led to chaos and physical hazard. *Perinde
Ac Cadaver,* to obey like a corpse, was the motto of the
Jesuits. The Jewish religious normative system also
stressed the *Mitzvot—Maassiot*—the routine rules of
behavior and ritual. These were considered far more important than abstract and scholastic ideologies.

Durkheim was literally a product of the Judaeo-
Christian tradition. He substituted the group-society for
God in his dogmatic justification of solidarity, and like
St. Simone, in his own way tried to construct a religion
of society. He contrasted the secure togetherness of the
tradition-bound *Gemeinschaft* with the impersonal
Gesellschaft, and put his faith in secure normative boun-
daries. As long as these are intact, the contents of social

processes may be varied and many; but if the boundaries are disrupted, chaos sets in. *Anomie,* a word Durkheim coined to denote the normative disintegration of society, is triggered by sudden and violent change. Conditions— for example, excessive affluence or want that injure the social and normative structure of society—invariably affect the well-being, safety, and survival of the individual. The Fiddler on the Roof who sings the praises of tradition, and B. F. Skinner, who advocates social control and deplores permissiveness, both echo Durkheim: When the normative system of society is intact, violence in words and actions may occur in passing; but when everything is permitted and individuals are alienated from their group, society becomes a self-defeating venture.

A different value judgment underlies the ideas of the conflict theorists, especially Georg Simmel and Lewis Coser (5). For them, tradition and the conservation of structures for romantic or pragmatic reasons leads to staleness and decadence, and admirably serves the purposes of tyranny. Rejecting Durkheim, they view adjustment and stability as negatives. Instead, they favor the Hegelian and Marxist brand of dialectics. Hegel viewed active struggle as the primary means by which the individual could overcome the rift between himself and his surroundings, while Marx said that, "It is the bad side that produces the movement that makes history by producing a struggle." For the conflict theorists any disruption of a steady state is better than a standstill. The synthesis resulting from a clash of conflicting forces is the essence of progress—the advance toward a better future. Consequently, they view deviance differently from Durkheim and his followers.

A value judgment diametrically opposite to Durkheim's is at the basis of the Existentialist social philosophy. Sartre postulates that social images created by the "common man," the mass media, and the "generalized others" of the social institutions cannot be grasped and comprehended subjectively by individuals. These social images that drive, move, and direct the individual cannot be perceived or experienced by him as a meaningful part of himself but only as lifeless vectors, an inauthentic, objectified, driving force. To Sartre the only human reality in existence lies in the subjective consciousness and conception of the self, which is the only source of transcendence ("If God is dead, Man is God"), as well as the only basis of values (6). Ego can never be subjectively conscious of others; he is a mere object to their subjective consciousness. Ego's presence limits and obstructs alter's freedom and self-consciousness, and *vice versa.* The result of this multiphasic limitation and obstruction is that most of the interaction and interrelations among human beings are initiated and terminated by fear, shame, pride, and vanity; social life is characterized, according to Sartre, by an endless and agonizing conflict. The only truly existing entity is the individual. Others, at best, are nauseating; and social solidarity (if it exists at all) is based on amorphous, vague, and negative (from the individual's point of view) values.

Sartre and his existentialist colleagues consequently evaluate group solidarity in a totally different way from Durkheimian sociologists. Also, in a society dominated by existentialist ideas, behavior labeled as deviant might be the proper thing to do in Middletown, U.S.A.

The Relativity of Deviance

Social deviance is relative—that is, it varies greatly with place and time, because the norms that define deviance are also relative. Almost every crime proscribed in our laws has been permitted or even considered commendable in other locations and other eras. Incest was practiced in ancient Egypt; patricide was normative among the Eskimos; and those who did not avail themselves of the services of the sacred prostitutes in ancient Canaan would have been deviant.

Suicide illustrates the relativity of deviance very well, because society is rarely indifferent about it. Judas Iscariot's suicide, for example, was regarded as a greater sin than his betrayal of Christ (7). According to Jewish religious law, a suicide is buried outside the boundaries of the cemetery. On moral grounds, suicides may be condemned as cowards, irresponsible people who have abandoned dependents without protection and security. A group may be less inclined to regard suicide as deviant in cases where identification with the suicide's act is possible—if, for instance, a man kills himself because he suffers from an incurable disease.

9

Some suicides are normative: hara kiri; suicide by those who have been offended and humiliated; and suicides of the servants and slaves of a deceased master. The mandatory suicide of Socrates was normative. So was Hitler's unsuccessful attempt to persuade his friend Ernest Rohm, who became politically expendable, to shoot himself in his prison cell. So also are those heroic suicides, who may become the subjects of national epics—the Japanese Kamikaze pilots, and the defenders of Massada, who preferred mass suicide to being captured alive by the Romans. In this last case, Josephus Flavius was considered a deviant because he preferred to live rather than die with his comrades.

Another fact that illustrates the relativity of deviance is that people who retreat from society and its norms—drug addicts, alcoholics, the clochards under the bridges of the Seine, the hobos in New York's Bowery, and vagabonds all over the world are viewed differently by various societies. Retreatists are regarded today as rejects, as outsiders and deviants who are not able to adjust to the demands of achievement-oriented social norms. However, in medieval Europe, escapists and retreatists could lose themselves with society's approval in monasteries; in 1100, in France alone, there were 540 monasteries. A Carthusian monastery offered each monk a secluded cell where he worked, ate, and slept alone, in almost uninterrupted silence. The clochard was not then regarded as a deviant; all he had to do was to join one of the holy orders of mendicants, after which he could drift and tramp around not only with impunity, but with the aura of a saint.

The Labeling Process

A third basic premise is that social deviance is strongly related to the group's reaction against a certain act and its perpetrator. The behavior of an individual is indeed important for his being considered a deviant; however, the crucial fact is that the group and its organs of social control may or may not label him as a deviant. This means that a given behavior outside its social context is insufficient to constitute social deviance. Many times people who are not at all deviant in their behavior have been labeled as such by the agencies of social control. The ostracizers in ancient Greece, the medieval inquisitors, and modern professional slanderers have caused people to be treated as deviants by authoritatively declaring that they are so. This illustrates W. I. Thomas's basic theorem of the social sciences, namely, that if Man defines a situation as real, it becomes real in its consequences. The branding mechanisms of society are the crucial instruments that create social deviance.

The nature of the labels is also highly relevant. The whole concept of deviance changes depending on the attitude of the group toward the deviant. It may regard the person who has infringed the norms as a sinner possessed by the devil, as a freak of nature, as a sick person, or as a normal human being who has learned to be bad. The attitude of the group toward criminals, for instance, has shifted throughout the ages. Originally, the criminal who offended against his fellow man was considered a sinner whose crime offended the gods and who was therefore polluted. This pollution was deemed to be contagious; the stigmatized offender was very often segregated and ostracized. Frazer (8) cites the fact that in ancient Attica, murderers were ostracized and outlawed, and anyone could injure or kill them with impunity. If another trial was pending against a murderer, he could return to defend himself, but he had to do so on board a boat while the judges conducted the trial on the seashore. The murderer was not allowed to touch land lest he pollute it and the people by contagion. Sanction was originally an expiatory act that was supposed to cleanse and purge this kind of pollution. Indeed, the word *punishment* (*peine* in French, *poena* in Latin, and *poine* in Greek) is derived from a Sanskrit root, meaning to cleanse and purify. Formal punishment cleanses the offender of his pollution and also appeases the gods; many stories in mythology, drama, and history illustrate this view. Expiatory rites eventually crystalized into our modern legal sanctions (9).

In certain historical periods, heresy has been used as a sanction applied to modes, beliefs, and behavior that were considered deviant. Heretics seem to have deviated not so much from the prevalent religious dogma, as from the norms of society relating to everyday life from accepted use of language, dress, manners, sexual mores, or external appearance and behavior (10). Stigmatization as a heretic was an extremely stiff sanction; heretics could consider themselves fortunate if they were merely ordered to wear a yellow cross on their garments (11). They suffered far worse fates at the hands of the Inquisition.

In modern society the sanction of a stigma differs in

kind and consequences from the medieval stigma of heresy, but its inherent nature is unchanged. An individual who is considered different in a way that infringes on the group's normative system is liable to be stigmatized as deviant. The social and economic consequences of this stigma depend on the severity of the infringement of the norm, and are determined by the inner strength of the norm, as measured by the public's indignation when this norm is infringed. The stigma, therefore, is the best instrument for measuring the inner strength of a social norm; the more severe the stigma, the stronger the social norm.

When the Renaissance in Europe gave way to what is called the Age of Reason, the focus of the group and the agencies of social control shifted from the sinful, polluted deviant to the criminal act itself. The classic school of Penal Philosophy concentrated on the offensive act as manifestation of the deviant's "badness" (12). The Judaeo-Christian concept of freedom of the will led to a view of the offense as a malicious act perpetrated out of a free choice to do bad, and provoked an eye for an eye reprisal for the offending act, regardless of attenuating or aggravating circumstances relating to the deviant's personality.

Next, society's attitude toward the deviant changed from condemning him as bad to treating him as sick or mad. By the end of the nineteenth century, Darwinian ideas of evolution had begun to influence behavioral and social scientists. This biological approach to deviancy, aided by a positivistic passion for measurement and data collection, meant that the criminal and deviant were regarded as atavistic freaks of nature. In Europe, disciples of Cesare Lombroso measured the cranial bones of murderers. Lange preached his "crime-as-destiny" theory, based on his findings about the preponderance of deviant identical twins over fraternal twins (13). And Kretschmer postulated his criminal body types (14). In America, Drahms measured the lengths of fingers and the cephalic widths of inmates of San Quentin (15). Mohr and Gundlack applied Kretschmer's physical typologies to the inmates of Joliet (16), while, at Harvard, Hooton worked on his neo-Lombrosian theories (17). Goring measured the height, physical makeup, and weight of 3000 English convicts (18, 19). He found juvenile delinquents to be physically small, and more undernourished than nondelinquents of the same ages. Schlapp and Smith, two German endocrinologists who studied hormonal secretions, explained that deviance in the second generation of immigrants was due to endocrinological disturbances in their mothers caused by their long journeys.

Today the Lombrosian approach to criminology, with its biophysiological reasons for crime, has been abandoned. As one biologist has said (20):

> Behavior defined as criminal does not render such behavior abnormal from either the biological or the social viewpoint. It merely renders it socially undesirable, and its undesirability is emphasized by the punishments which are prescribed for its expression, and which are supposed to serve as deterrents to its performance. From the standpoint of the biologist it is, nonetheless, perfectly normal behavior.

This is a fact which, when judgments of "criminal" behavior are made, is often neglected. Many students of crime tend rather to approach the study of criminal behavior as if such behavior were in itself abnormal, as if there were something intrinsically "wrong" with the organism exhibiting this "wrong" behavior. The persistent and practically serious error committed here is, quite unjustifiably, to translate a judgment of social value into one of biological value. Much of the thinking and writing about crime, in America as in Europe, is vitiated by this serious error. It is this error which has to a large extent been responsible for the belief that there exists some relation between criminal behavior and the biological structure of the organism.

Somewhat related to the biological approach is the view that the deviant is mentally twisted or sick. Many studies have tried to link crime and deviance to psychosis (21), neurosis (22), mental retardation (23), the vague syndrome of psychopathy, (24), and assorted personality pecularities (25). Most sociologists today, however, consider that crime and deviance are "normal," that is, they are not necessarily related to personality pathology. This point of view, which was elaborated by the late Edwin Sutherland and his followers (26), assumes no significant differences in the prevelance of structural personality defects between deviants and the population at large. There would be similar distribution, for instance, of neuroses, hot tempers, timidity, aggressiveness, and stable personalities among the Cosa Nostra families, the British Horticultural Association, the Rotary Club of Tel Aviv, and the New York Chamber of Commerce.

Instead, contemporary sociological theory links most criminal or socially deviant behavior to learning processes. A child may be socialized, for example, by criminal parents or siblings, or even by whole communities like the Indian criminal tribes. A child who is brought up this way learns the art of picking pockets together with his tribal dialect. In most cases, however, the learning of criminal and deviant patterns of behavior is preceded by alienation from the prevailing value systems. Indeed, even opiate addiction is believed to develop through cognitive conditions (27). By excluding biophysiological and psychopathological factors, this viewpoint makes crime and deviance social by interactive phenomena which are culturally transmitted or induced through identification, association, conditioning, and other learning processes.

Mental Diseases as Social Deviance

This recent trend to regard functional (as distinct from the organically caused) mental illness as a breakdown in human interaction justifies its inclusion as a form of social deviance. Here again, societal reactions to mental aberration very much determine its nature and outward manifestations.

In ancient times, certain forms of insanity were considered a divine affliction; epilepsy was for many centuries called "the sacred disease." At the same time, however, the insane were also considered criminals, vagabonds, pariahs, and outlaws, whose deviation from society's normative systems was conclusive proof of their communion with the devil (28). All those who were conspicuously different were heretics; and the insane were manifestly different in their behavior and their conception of reality. As Gregory Zilboorg said, "Every mental patient either aggressively rejects life as we like it—and was therefore thought of as a heretic, witch or sorcerer; or he passively succumbs to his inability to accept life as we see it—and was therefore called bewitched" (29).

As in criminology, no physiological correlate has been found at the basis of functional psychosis. Now and again someone attempts to link functional personality defects with biophysiological factors, but so far the most we can say is that any casual link between biological factors and nonorganic mental aberration has yet to be proved. Harry Stack Sullivan contended that, "persons showing mental disorder do not manifest anything specifically different in kind from what is manifested by practically all human beings" (30). The contemporary approach that regards functional psychoses as breakdowns of interaction between the insane individual and other human beings reflects Sullivan's view that schizophrenia is not a disease entity but a "grave disorder of living" (31). Indeed, all the manifestations of the functional psychoses have been considered at other times, in other places, and in other cultures as normative behavior, fashionable, commendable, or even as proof of divine visitation (32). We may therefore define a functional psychosis in sociocultural terms as a process incidental to interpersonal communication and interaction which is labeled as morbid in a given cultural context (33). This definition accords with Halmos's ingenious observation that, "cultures vary according to the degree of abnormality they encourage and legitimize" (34). The societal reaction to a given human condition, and not this condition or behavior per se, define it as morbid for the individual patient and his relevant others. The neuroses and the lesser personality aberrations, too, may be regarded as socially deviant behavior insofar as clinicians single them out as needing treatment. In terms of social deviance, this amounts to urging neurotics to be cured so that their behavior will conform more closely to the prevailing social norms.

The Scope of Social Deviance

The justifications for conformity are many, ranging from Hobbes' view that laws are a safeguard against man acting as wolf to his fellow men, to the Judaic maxim that commendable behavior is paid for by more of the very same behavior: conformity is good in itself. Plato advocated rules because they sustain beauty and harmony; Nietzche asserted that when everything is possible, nothing is true; and Durkheim viewed conformity as synonymous with group cohesion, solidarity, and morality.

We have considerable factual evidence that human beings tend to conform to group norms. Studies on conformity by Sheriff and Asch, for instance, show that individuals tend to renounce their own factually correct perception and adjust to the collusionary erroneous view of the group because of their wish to conform to the group. Bogdonoff and his associates even found a physiological correlate to conformity. They observed in an Asch-type perceptual conformity study that the non-conformist had a high level of fatty acids, indicating an anxiety-correlated arousal of the central nervous system, whereas the conformists had a low acid level indicating a relaxed nervous system and well-being (35). (George Orwell in *1984*, describes Winston as suddenly feeling relaxed and happy when he agrees to the statement that two plus two equals five.)

Other studies of the so-called Stoner effect also show that individual perceptions tend to become congruent with the perception of the whole group after individual judgments have been openly compared and discussed by the group (36). And this tendency to conform has also been found by Crutchfield and others to be linked to personality traits in a way that can be measured (37).

This tendency of individuals to conform to group norms has been related to a human longing for congruity. Philosophers from Parmenides onward have regarded this longing as axiomatic; and in the social and behavioral sciences, it has been the basis for elaborate theoretical models. Newcomb, for instance, introduced into social psychology what he calls an individual's "strain toward symmetry." Presumably, congruity and symmetry may be regarded as special instances of a deeper harmony that is inherent in unity.

The human tendency to conform may be responsible not only for the gradual suppression of some forms of deviance, but also for the institutionalization of deviant groups and deviant patterns of behavior. The prostitute, the operator of an illegal gambling house, and the drug pusher supply commodities that are readily consumed by a considerable segment of the population; however, as long as they are stigmatized by society, they are regarded, and in most cases see themselves, as deviants. On the other hand, hippies' modes of behavior—long hair, say, or marihuana smoking—cease to be deviant because their adoption by wider groups gives them a dimension of social change.

It is even possible that some deviant groups may become acceptable to the majority *because* of their deviancy—for instance, Bohemian artist colonies may become tourist attractions, and their exotic deviancy turned into a commodity sold to the squares. Often, these areas become an asset to the socio-economic structure, and many of their inhabitants for business reasons slavishly conform to middle-class concept of the outsider—professional deviants who turn their deviant mannerisms into a commodity, and who do their utmost to augment their social visibility. The crucial point is that both the institutionalized deviants themselves and the rest of society regard them as an integral part of the social structure, and the institutionalized deviant thus preaches stylized subversion under the auspices of a social structure that he does not seriously mean to destroy. The salon communist, the salon radical, and the salon hippie may advocate fiery rebellion, but they always take pains to adhere to whichever rebellious movement happens to be "in" at the time. Apparently one of the surest ways to be accepted by society is to defy it in a not too injurious manner.

Some social structures incorporate types of deviance simply because they have no other choice. A case in point is the use of the tap in the aircraft industry. This instrument is illegal, because its use weakens the alignments between nuts and bolts in the aircraft. On the other hand, it speeds up production, and therefore helps the workers to earn more money and the management to produce more airplanes. As a result, the use of the tap is widespread, although formally it is considered as a "criminal instrument" (38). This kind of deviation from standards is very common.

On the basis of what has been said so far, we may define social deviance as a disjunction between the roles and expectations of the individual and the roles and expectations of the group. Deviance may result either from purposeful behavior of the individual, or from some structural properties of the group, and both individuals and groups may be deviant. A single individual may deviate from the norms of his membership group, or the normative system of society at large. Groups—for example, criminal subcultures—may deviate from the norms of the larger society of which they are a part, even though the individuals comprising the criminal subculture are conformists to the deviant normative system of their group. Deviancy is relative to a specific set of norms, because even the most hardened member of a criminal group conforms to a great many norms of his society and to many laws of the state to which he belongs.

We must also distinguish between the deviant act and the deviant character (39). All members of groups do commit, from time to time, deviant acts, but to be labeled deviant, one has to engage in deviance in a more than casual manner. The deviant person may therefore be identified by the frequency and severity of norm infringement, and legal labeling of the professional criminal or the habitual deviant is formal and conspicuous. As far as the sporadic or accidental deviant is concerned, however, it is difficult to decide whether an act, or series of acts, is deviant, or whether the person himself should be considered a deviant character.

The study of social deviance entails integrating sociological, legal, and psychological aspects of behavior. I propose to analyze this complex subject by discussing the phenomenology of social deviance—its description and appearance: its functional qualities—its properties and consequences; and its causation—the "whys" that explain how deviance occurs, and the factors that are associated with it.

Moral Standards such as those expressed in the
Ten Commandments are described as being promulgated
merely for the convenience of those who have some
interest to protect, as for example, property owners—
"Thou shalt not steal"—and persons who have sexual
partners—"Thou shalt not commit adultery." Thus
B attempts to change the basis for A's performing
the behavior from doing B a personal favor to
satisfying social or moral obligations.

L E D ANTEC

CHAPTER **II**

THE

NORMS

The Nature of Social Norms

As social deviance is the infringement of social norms, we must first examine the nature of these norms. Thibaut and Kelley define norms as "agreements or consensus about the behavior [that] group members should or should not enact, and social processes to produce adherence to this agreement" (1). Legal norms are an integral part of the over-all normative system in a given society; as far as content is concerned, there is no material difference between a legal norm and other social norms. Some criminal acts are similar in crime content to the kind of civil actions that stem from negligent behavior—for instance, in motor accidents; and behavior in business, politics, and administration which is described as white-collar crime can be very similar to infringements of the criminal law, but is not included within it for formal reasons.

The distinction between the criminal law and other social norms lies in the way in which legal norms are enforced as part of the system of social control. In other words, the specific reaction society exhibits toward the infringements of the legal norm is the criterion for distinguishing it from other social norms. Criminal law norms thus differ from other social norms in the way they are enforced and in the consequences of their enforcement. The punitive aspect in the sanction of the legal norm puts it on an altogether different level from the norms that are sanctioned by ridicule, scorn, gossip, or ostracism. The ritualistic elements in the criminal procedure, the special setting of the courtroom, the necessity to plead guilty or not guilty, the formal conviction, the publicity that ensues, and the stigma that conviction carries separate the criminal law norm from the other social norms. Furthermore, violators of legal norms *must* participate (if caught, of course) in the criminal trial; in this respect, too, the criminal law norm is unique.

Norms are mandates imposed by the group. Their acquisition by the human individual involves a continuous process of learning or "socialization." The infant of course has no conception of the values of his society. During the early years, parents are responsible for discipline and control of children. The child of two or three has developed no specific moral controls, and has no sense of right or wrong except in terms of a self-related reference. Something is right if it provides for his satisfaction and pleasure or relief of tension; something is wrong if it hurts him or causes pain. His response to something wrong is to retaliate or protest. The basic moral law of the young child is simply the *lex talionis*— an eye for an eye. "If you hit me, I'll hit you back."

Such self-centered behavior makes for anarchy, and increasingly as the child grows, parental discipline sets certain limits. The child learns that he cannot always have what he wants when he wants it, and that there must be respect for other people, if only because he is going to be hurt when he transgresses acceptable limits. The child tends to absorb the standards of those about him. This process of socialization, the incorporation of parental and social values, is a process that takes place throughout childhood. At the start, the process is concrete and mechanical—that is, the child complies with parental rules because the parents have the authority to back up those rules. In due course, he achieves an autonomous ethical system, tested through a process of trial and error, by which he weighs his conduct according to his own inner standards.

Freud observed that there is a period crucial for the incorporation of an inner value system that occurs around the age of five or six. He related it to the child's forming a more specific sense of identity as a boy or a girl, which involves the child's developing a sense of his or her role in the family; he also related it to the oedipal events of these years. The boy who has selfishly wanted to have his mother all to himself is forced to recognize at this age that his father has the inside track. The boy eventually gives up competing with his father, and instead identifies with him, making his father's values a part of himself. A comparable process takes place in the young girl. Essentially, it is at this period that the child develops an inner sense of rules, a conscience, a sense of right and wrong; after this age, therefore, he has inner controls which are not just related to parental correction. These inner controls are refined as the child grows older, and especially during adolescence as the young person retests society's rights and wrongs, and through social role experimentation works toward establishing an adult identity.

In adolescence, adult values must be challenged and tested in order for the individual to prove that he has a separate identity and is capable of independent action. This challenge to adult values may be done on an individual basis, but it is more commonly experienced within adolescents groups or gangs. Gang membership provides a sense of security and strength which permits a youth to act in a way that he could not do on his own (2). The gang provides a challenge to the family unit; but it also provides security and establishes simple and consistent norms where values are sharply defined in black and white, without ambiguities.

Adolescence, then, is a period of crisis; if the crisis is not overcome properly, a predisposition to crime, violence, or deviance may be the result. It is not unlike a childhood disease which everyone has to get, but which may involve serious complications. If the socialization in the family prior to or within this critical period has been faulty, the adolescent will not have any strong and clear normative barriers against deviant solutions to life problems.

Ragmar Rommetveit has proposed a very useful way to systematize the processes that lead to conformity to social norms. He analyzed the transmission and enforcement of norms by the group (norm sending) and the degree to which the norms have been received and internalized by the individual (3). The norm-sending process requires first of all a statement by the group as to the desired behavior and the consequences to the individual if he does not comply. The group must then maintain surveillance over the person in order to determine the extent (if any) of his compliance to the norm. Lastly the group must apply sanctions to noncomplying individuals.

The degrees of individual conformity to the norm are graded from mere compliance, where the individualis induced to conform by constant surveillance and by the threat of negative, that is, depriving sanctions; through identification, where conforming behavior is induced by positive, that is, rewarding sanction and conformity becomes, thus, autonomously rewarding; to internalization of the norm by the individual, which is complete conformity. Surveillance and sanction are not necessary with internalization because the internalized norm, when incorporated by the individual as a personality element, becomes "just," "right," and "true."

Norm-sending and norm-receiving describes not only the processes of socialization, but also the structure of social norms. However, the content of norms is also relevent in any analysis of conformity and deviance.

Social norms may be regarded as anything between two extremes, ranging from triviality on one hand to being more important than life itself, on the other. The content of the norm determines whether a given infringement is important enough to justify a reaction (sanction); it also determines the magnitude of the reaction. Consequently, the strength of a norm is very closely related to its content. The task of measuring the strength of a norm is by no means easy. Sellin, in his classic monograph, *Culture-Conflict and Crime,* proposed the idea of measuring the strength of norms by their "resistance potential." He said, "A conduct norm is a rule which governs a specific type of life situation and is authoritative to the extent of the group's resistance to its violation. The inherent energy or power of the norm may be called its resistance potential" (4). The group's reaction to the violation of a norm may be predicted from its attitude toward the violators and the nature of the derogatory tag (stigma) with which he is labeled. We may therefore substitute the strength of the stigma, which is more readily measurable than Sellin's resistance potential, as an index of the inner strength of the norm. Indeed, the only way to measure the resistance potential is by the apparent reaction of the group to the infringement of the norm.

Transmission of Norms

The strength of a norm is naturally very much dependent on how effectively it has been transmitted and promulgated. Defects in the process of norm-sending may occur in each of its three phases. The statement of the norm may be unclear, ambiguous or contain overt or latent contradictions. When the norm-sending occurs in the primary socialization agencies—family, school, church—the statement of rules may be clouded by conflicts stemming from disparate views of parents and attitudes toward authority, private property, education, and the use of violence; any of these conflicts might contribute to forming the children's attitude toward deviant or nondeviant behavior. There may also be conflict in the transmission of norms within the family as a result of discord between parents and children, an inconsistent degree of parental discipline, or discord over values and norms between the parents and other socializing agencies such as school, church, and clubs.

The effectiveness of norm sending may be enhanced by the prestige of the norm source. If the infringer of a norm has high status and prestige, others are more apt to follow his example in violating the norm. One study showed that when a traffic signal was ignored by a high-status pedestrian attired in a freshly pressed suit, shined shoes, white shirt and a tie, a higher number of other pedestrians also ignored the red light than when the same man behaved in the same way dressed in soiled, patched trousers, scuffed shoes, and a blue denim shirt (5). Conversely, an injury to the prestige of the source of the norms hampers the norm-sending. This may be seen in communities that undergo a rapid or sudden social change, and especially within immigrant families whose original cultural tradition is markedly different from the culture of the absorbing community and who have undergone socioeconomic injuries that have shattered the status of the head of the family.

This type of social change blurs the rules because it creates conflicts within the family between the immigrant parents and their native-born offspring (or those who came very young). The reason is that the family is a system in balance. Every time this balance is disturbed, every time the family boat is rocked, the way the child absorbs the parental mandates for conduct is bound to be affected. For the child tends to absorb within his personality the whole family image as reflected to him by the elaborate and subtle inter-relationships among the family members (6). In addition, the many patterns of reciprocity between parent and child also affect socialization. Psychiatrists have described what they call the "symbiotic" relationships between parent and child. An aggressive mother, for instance, may make her child a receptacle for her aggression; conversely, a guilt-ridden and self-blaming mother may unconsciously solicit aggression from her children (7). It follows, therefore, that factors which influence the strength or weakness of the equilibrium of the family system may also affect the transmission of conduct norms to the young; and therefore, a loosely-knit family will be a less effective organ of socialization than a tight-knit and cohesive family (8). Whether the mother is employed outside the house is an important factor in the child's enculturazation (9). So, too, are the nature of the father's occupation (10) and the quality of the family's housing (11).

More general defects in the transmission of norms, legal and non-legal, may occur between institutions within society when there is a communication breakdown between the norm-senders and the actual or potential norm-receivers. These communication gaps may very often be observed in technologically backward countries, and those into which many people have migrated. In these cases, the norm-sending process is completely inefficient because the people remain quite ignorant of the existence of the norms to which they are supposed to conform. It is futile and tedious for a magistrate in a rural area in Egypt to try to administer justice in villages where the Fellahins never hear about laws passed in Cairo. Similar problems occur among Bedouins who may not know that city laws do not allow avenging the blood of a murdered brother, or among mountain Jews from Morocco who do not know that Israeli laws prescribe life imprisonment for killing a daughter who becomes pregnant out of wedlock. These are extreme examples; but many laws are passed which do not reach those they are meant to affect. The norm-sending process does not even begin to operate simply because individuals never begin to hear about it.

The danger in this situation is that the present trend toward state control of fields from economy to education—not only in the totalitarian and welfare states, but also in the capitalistic ones—results in a continuous flow of laws, decrees, and rules and does subject the individual quite often to inconsistent pressures. Too many bureaucratic rules and regulations create multiple conflicts, and are apt to leave the individual in utter confusion as to what the rules are, who stated them, and when and where they are to be observed. This danger of too many norms that regulate life situations has been discussed by Thibaut and Kelley: "Under these conditions [too many norms], said to characterize bureaucracies, the rules governing behavior can be so complex that people are unable to master them fully. The result is an unwillingness to act or make behavioral decisions. The individual may also become so engrossed with the internal structure and interpretations of the norms that he loses touch with the outside world" (12).

Surveillance and Sanctions

Norm-sending may also be deficient as far as surveillance and application of sanctions. Normative indoctrination in the family has very little reciprocity. Mostly it is a unilateral flow of authority and power from the parents to their children. However, in families where the mother is the principal disciplinarian, children tend to develop guilt (that is, to internalize norms) more readily than when the father performs the main tasks of surveillance (13). Also, there is evidence that middle-class children are more likely to adopt their parents' occupational and educational goals than children in working and lowerclass families (14).

The third and most crucial phase of norm transmission is the application of sanctions: punishment for noncompliance, and rewards for compliance. One of the main ways we acquire norms is through conditioning; that is, we can be taught to conform because, like rats in a maze, we naturally refrain from actions that are associated with pain, and prefer to behave in ways that are reinforced by rewarding experiences. When sanctions are sporadic, erratic, and inconsistent, however, conditioning does not take place, and norm transmission may be poor.

Over-severe punitive sanctions are also detrimental to norm internalization. Unusually severe or harsh child-rearing practices have been linked to poor and fragmentary norm-internalization (15). In like manner, overly-intense punishment seems to be ineffective in suppressing undesired behavior (16). Another study has indicated that children who have experienced rejection or extreme punitiveness from their parents are likely to show weak internalization of a sense of duty and responsibility, and to have poor control over their tendency to behave aggressively (17). A survey of delinquent adolescent gang members revealed that their parents were unusually punitive and rejecting (18). As Kohlberg, who has studied the development of morals, has noted (19):

> Parents of delinquents tend to be more punitive than parents of non-delinquents, although they do not differ in the extent of "firmness" of socialization and home demands. They are less warm and affectionate and more inconsistent and neglectful than parents of non-delinquents. Delinquent boys tend to have overtly hostile relationships with their fathers.

Conversely, when parents, and especially mothers are warm and affectionate to their infants, the efficacy of socialization is greatly enhanced. Consequently, it seems clear that withdrawal of affection, or the threat of withdrawal, is the most durable and effective sanction (20). The delay of reward as a sanction has also been most effective in suppressing undesirable behavior (21). Middle-class families resort more to withdrawal of affection as sanctions in socializing their children than do the lower classes who inflict more repressive punishment (22). This may partly explain the lower incidence of violence-delinquency and norm-violation in general among middle-class youths whose socialization was presumably more effective.

Inequality Before the Law

The prevailing view in many societies, and especially among the underprivileged classes, is that equality before the law is largely a myth. As Daniel Drew, a shady business associate of the nineteenth-century robber barons, once declared, "Law is like a cobweb; it's made for flies and the smaller kinds of insects, so to speak, but lets the big bumblebees break through" (23). But differential treatment of lawbreakers—that is, differences in surveillance of compliance, and the application of sanctions—has a shattering effect on the norm-sending process. For instance, differential law enforcement frequently occurs in cases of white-collar crime, which may be defined as the criminality of the upper socioeconomic classes in relation to business, politics, and the professions.

Sutherland has demonstrated (24) huge number of offences by large corporations, from defrauding of shareholders to the submission of false financial reports. The food industry sells some products which do not meet legal specifications, and may actually be injurious to health. Bribery is practiced by many corporations as an integral part of routine business. Politics is riddled with graft, employees embezzle corporate funds, and advertising campaigns lie about the quality of the product. The point here is that white-collar criminals are treated differently from other criminals by the law-enforcement agencies. This is clear to everyone, and severely vitiates the effect of norms that proscribe white-collar offences. Indeed, the effect of this relative immunity of the white-collar crime perpetrators both to detection and prosecution on the norm-sending process is to enhance cynical attitudes toward the law and law enforcement agencies, and to promote suspicion, and bitterness toward agencies of government and authority as a whole. Ordinary crimes—burglary, theft, and violence—are committed by persons who are in many ways outside the law-abiding society. They are clearly stigmatized as criminals, and sooner or later are forced to become part of the criminal subculture. White-collar criminals, on the other hand, as a rule belong to respectable circles, and to a community's social elite; when this elite not only commits grave offences against the state, the economy, and the public at large, but also gets away with it, the public (lower-class and middle-class alike) will inevitably begin to distrust and belittle the entire legal system.

A similar injurious effect on the efficacy of norm-sending is caused by the "fix." The fix is closely associated with the influence of organized crime on law-enforcement agencies, especially when chiefs of police, district attornies, and judges are elected officials. A whole class of persons who have the appropriate connections with the political machines are able to escape prosecution by having their cases fixed (25)—that is, dropped. A similar bad effect on the norm-sending process is caused by legislation that is passed that serves the interests of a powerful minority as opposed to the interests of the population at large: laws designed to favor big business and industry, for example, over the interests of the consumers.

Another phenomenon that tends to injure and weaken the norm-sending process of the legal system as a whole is the relatively low rate of detection of offences. According to one report, this rate for serious offences some years ago was around 23 per cent (26). In 2,000 cities in the U.S. for the year 1958 (27), the rates of reported offences cleared by arrest were as follows: murder, 94 per cent; rape, 73 per cent; aggravated assault, 79 per cent; robberies, 43 per cent; burglaries, 30 per cent; larcenies, 20 per cent.

The data in 1967 provided by the President's Commission on Law Enforcement and Administration of Justice, indicated that aggravated assaults and larcenies of over 50 dollars occurred twice as often as they were reported; that is, there are 50 per cent more robberies than are reported. In some areas the Commission found only one-tenth of the total number of crimes were reported to the police. Seventy-four per cent of the neighborhood commercial establishments surveyed did not report to police the thefts committed by their employees. The average percentage of arrests ranged from 91 for homicide to 20 for larceny (28).

This low rate for the detection of some types of offence, and particularly of offences against property —which are the most frequent of the offences committed in most societies—injures the efficient promulgation of the norm that "crime does not pay," because apparently it does. Furthermore, faulty, irregular, and discriminatory surveillance and application of sanctions may also tend to augment the rates of this particular norm-infringement, because an increase in behavior that is contrary to some norms leads to the realization (which is used also as a rationalization after the act) that "everybody's doing it."

Researchers in communication have pointed out some factors that are applicable to the over-all efficacy of norm-sending. For instance, the machinery of norm-sending may become clogged when the sources of norms are overcommitted and saturated—a harassed traffic coordinator during a traffic light breakdown. In an overcentralized system of norm-sending, some peripheral norm-sources may become ineffective—a rule-setting committee in a remote rural area in Red China that has to apply to Peking for instructions about every minor decision. Stressing the positive advantages of a norm is a more effective way to transmit it than pointing out the negative aspects of infringing it. And if the group that is the source of the norm is unanimously against a dissenter, he will be brought back into conformity far more effectively than if his dissenting stance is supported by some individuals within the norm-sending group itself (29).

Internalization of Norms

As far as norm-receiving is concerned, various factors are linked to the depth or strength of norm internalization. Internalization of a single norm or a group of norms may be made more effective by weaving it or them into a comprehensive system. This technique has been used by every scholastic system, from the Catholic Church to the teachings of Chairman Mao. Another potent way to enhance internalization of norms is by personalizing them, so that the perceiver feels that the transmission is directed toward him personally. "God loves you and wants you to do good." "Big Brother is watching you!" "Uncle Sam needs you!" and he points his finger directly at you.

A person's self-esteem and self-assurance are effective barriers against attempts to persuade him or her to change an attitude. Conversely, when self-esteem is shattered, or a person is subjected to degrading institutional routines or prolonged social isolation, these events may weaken the previously held normative ideas, and thereby facilitate his acceptance of the contradictory norms. A potent barrier against this kind of persuasion is inoculation, some training and exposure to contradictory norms and ideas, so that the person gains some practice in defending his beliefs. Practice also develops the motivation to defend a normative stance; there is no reason to defend a norm one believes is invulnerable (30). A Talmudic scholar must be conversant with the doctrines of heresy; otherwise he may not be able to refute the blasphemies of an apostate.

Finally, the strength of a norm is dependent on the individual's state of mind. A strong norm is one that is subjectively defined as relevant and important enough for him to sustain any strain when it conflicts with other norms. A subjective view of relevance varies, of course, with each individual as he grows older.

I find then a law, that, when I would
do good, evil is present within me.

SAINT PAUL:
Romans, 7, 21

CHAPTER **III**

THE

MANY

FACES

OF

DEVIANCE

The Phenomenology of Deviance

The phenomenology of deviance is mostly studied from the individual's point of view, whereas the structural expositions of the Durkheimian tradition take the group as a unit of analysis. This point is relevant for the correct evaluation of such structural analyses of deviance as Merton's essay on "Social Structure and Anomie." On the face of it, Merton deals with the various types of individual deviance; but a closer analysis reveals that Merton is describing the adaptations of individuals to the conflicts between the social structure and its corresponding normative system (1). Also most, if not all, structural expositions of deviance, anomie, and alienation from Durkheim, through Merton and Parsons, to Seeman and others, deal with value deviation and deviant behavior as one entity. At most they regard value deviation as a predisposing factor to deviant behavior. However, a phenomenological analysis must distinguish between deviant behavior and value deviation, which deals with the individual's detachment from the value system of the group and which may not have any overt manifestations.

A third phenomenological factor of deviance stems from the contention that human behavior out of its cultural context is neutral. The tagging, the labeling, the commendable attributes, or the derogatory stigma are crucial factors in identifying an act as bad or good, conforming or deviant. The model thus is:

Value Deviation + Deviant Behavior + Social Stigma → Social Deviance

In other words, stigma, deviant behavior, and value deviation are interrelated with one another and are linked to social deviance in a descending order of significance. However, this model leaves out a factor that is significant in many deviant acts—that of faith ▪in transcendental powers. Take, for example, the behavior of Michael Denis Rohan, an Australian sheep shearer touring Israel who set fire to the Mosque of El-Aqsa in Jerusalem.

To claim that Rohan acted as he did because he was insane is too easy. Of course, he was mad; but to label him as psychotic hardly explains everything. There were many grim events in his history. His father was a cruel disciplinarian, his mother was mentally deranged, his sister was retarded, his brother a truant. One of his teachers once ordered the five-year old Denis to stand in the trash basket, while his classmates jeered. In this kind of environment, Rohan could never have become a successful businessman or a professor. Although evidently his early experiences predisposed him to a morbid and deviant career, Rohan's behavior also reflects his very strong religious beliefs. He had an egocentric faith in the Bible and Gospel as preached by the Radio Church of God; he also had hallucinations, and believed himself to be Christ the Branch, spoken of by the prophet Zechariah. These hallucinations were no doubt wholly psychopathological; nonetheless Rohan's fundamentalist adoption of biblical prophecies and his equating of the Resurrection of the Temple with ultimate salvation at least partly explain his behavior. He visited the Temple Mount and found the Mosque of El Aqsa there. How could the Temple be rebuilt—the task that the Branch was required to accomplish by the prophet—if the Mosque was in its place? First of all, obviously, the Mosque had to be destroyed, erased, burned down to make way for salvation. This is a simple, logical inference, based on the Bible as literal truth.

What Rohan's case, with all its bizarre improbabilities, shows us is that any model of deviance that excludes faith and other transcendental factors is bound to be incomplete. Deviance motivated by religion is not confined to a Rohan, to a Manson mesmerizing his followers into a murderous trance, or to a Genet performing a black mass in a desecrated cathedral. The deviant avenues to salvation are just a logical step away from conventional mysticism. This is borne out by the assertion of Being and the fusion of self with some transcendental ultimate experienced by deviants while performing an irreversible act, such as murder or arson.

Genet, for instance, glorifies the act of murder as a fusion of moral vigor, freedom, and fulfillment. The murderer displays moral vigor by accepting his destiny. Green-eyes, one of Genet's heroes, feels relaxed and calm after the murder that will lead him eventually to the guillotine, because all confusion about his identity has finally been clarified: he is the murderer. Such a liberating sense of freedom is always related to the dispersion of ambiguity about self-image. By taking a life, a person delineates his social contours and puts himself in touch with eternity. Genet preached that the ritual of murder should have the solemnity of a black mass. Manson, too, as evidenced by the Tate murders in Hollywood, felt that the ceremony of murder demands a rite of hatred.

Genet, the bastard, the foundling, finds ultimate meaning through his trinity of theft, homosexuality and betrayal. Manson, the illegitimate child, and lifelong truant, finds a new identity in preaching the gospel of murder to his harem.

The conception of psychosis, as a disease entity, not a flaw in human interaction, blurs the boundaries between the mad and the fanatic-eccentric. Rohan is no doubt an extreme case, but he differs only in degree and not in nature from the millions of fundamentalist believers who take the Scriptures literally. Faith is universal. The belief in God and a hereafter is only a small part of man's encounter with transcendence, for our entire conception of reality—things, flora, fauna, other human beings "out there"—is of necessity based on faith. So is our distinction between "good" and "bad." Transcendence, therefore, is a vital component in any explanation of sin or piety, and also of deviance and crime.

If a person comes to the conclusion that his existence is empty, devoid of reality and meaning, he may assert his existence by a negative act, such as murder or suicide, which has a basic ontological significance. These acts have been widely explored by novelists and dramatists, but hardly at all by behavioral and social scientists. Here again, any model of deviance must be deficient insofar as it excludes the playing of evil roles as an act of self-definition. For some types and on some levels of analysis, the ontological and transcendental correlates of deviance are quite relevant, if not indeed crucial. Additionally, the self-concept of an individual as a conformist or deviant may be related to many levels of awareness. When a person identifies himself with criminal roles or deviant images, he may try to explain the reason for this to himself. We may presume that a person rarely resorts to sociological or psychological theories of deviance in order to explain himself to himself: these are usually either unknown to him, or else they do not seem to apply to his life. More probably, he tries to find out why he is *different* from others, why

others regard him as an outcast, as an outsider, as bad—
and to look for the meaning of the events in which he
participates. When these prove to be puzzling or evasive,
he may conclude that they are not as important to him
as the fact of his conviction or prison sentence. The
language and the form this metaphysical and ontological introspection may take are not relevant. A
renegade priest may ask heaven and his tormentors,
unde malum? (why evil?), and the pimp may describe his
life in gutter language; but the message is the same.

On the basis of this reflection, let us add two components to our initial model of deviance. One is the inherent ontological conception of self; the second is the
concept of transcendence. The model will thus be as follows: Self-Concept + Value Deviance + Deviant
Behavior + Social Stigma + Transcendental Convictions → Social Deviance.

Let us analyze each component of this phenomenological model of deviance separately.

Self-Concept

According to some personality theories, self-
concept is gained through the individual's interactions
with his surroundings, especially with the relevant
others around him. The infant's needs for food, shelter,
and acceptance and the impossibility having these needs
met fully and constantly by the providers mean that

there is always a conflictual aspect to this interaction. The self-concept is delineated by the ego boundary, the imaginary dividing line between our self-concept and the outside world (2). This ego boundary does not exist in the very early phases of development. The young child does not clearly differentiate between himself, other human beings, and his inanimate surroundings. He learns to do this through interaction with his relevant others in early socialization. As his ability to distinguish grows stronger, the boundary between himself and the world becomes clearer, and his self-concept more distinct.

The idea that a strong ego boundary underlies a favorable self-image is a part of many theoretical and empirical expositions of deviance. One of the first theories of deviance, or, to be more precise, conformity in relation to the self-concept, was Reckless's containment theory (3). The gist of this theory is that internal containment consists of "self components" that are related to the strength of the self as an operating person. Internal containment is composed of:

    1. A favorable image of self in relation to other persons, groups, and institutions.

    2. An awareness of being an inner-directed, goal-oriented person.

    3. A high level of frustration tolerance. [That is, one does not lose one's cool very easily.]

    4. Strongly internalized morals and ethics.

This image of the strong, silent, reliable, and moral

man—very much like the heroes of American movies of the twenties and thirties—does indeed imply a self-concept, properly internalized, which is well-insulated against deviance. Subsequent research on inner barriers against delinquency has revealed, however, that "insulation against delinquency is an ongoing process reflecting internalization of non-delinquent values and conformity to the expectations of significant others." (4)

Glazer's differential identification theory deals with the absorption by the individual of deviant roles. Its essence is that "a person pursues criminal (or deviant) behavior to the extent that he identifies himself with real or imaginary persons from whose perspective his criminal behavior seems acceptable" (5). In other words, a person who incorporates within his self-concept deviant roles and images is more likely to behave in a deviant manner.

Sykes and Matza have discussed what they call "techniques of neutralization" by means of which a deviant may rationalize his motives for his behavior so that he retains a positive self-concept for having done the "right" thing (6). A delinquent may quote psychiatric literature, or *West Side Story* to prove that his personality has been molded by the wretchedness of slums, so that it would have been impossible for him to behave otherwise, and that consequently he is not morally responsible. He may also point out that because of the elaborate insurance systems nobody really suffers from a bank robbery. Or he may assert that homosexuals have it coming to them if they are mugged and robbed while looking for small boys in the park. Another common technique of neutralization is based on the belief that one's loyalty to the gang is more important than the laws of society. A gang member's self-concept of being right not only remains intact, but is actually strengthened when he prefers the norms of his deviant gang to the square rules of society.

There are some less-generalized ontological expositions of deviance based on specific and relatively well-defined modes of behavior. Cressey's study of embezzlers, for instance, shows that embezzlement is anchored in "unsharable problems" (7). These are conflicts between the potential embezzler's self-concept, as presented to relevant others, and the harsh facts of real life. A bank messenger who presents himself to his new girl friend as a bank manager cannot possibly explain expensive night club bills to his boss, just as a husband cannot share with his wife the news that he has lost a month's salary at the race track. Both might turn to embezzlement as the only way out of their plight.

The masculine protest theory was formulated by Talcott Parsons (8), and is based on his analysis of the structure of the middle-class American family. The mother is the main socializing figure in this family; the father most of the time is outside the home taking care of his business and other affairs. The boy's identification tends to be with the role-model of his mother; consequently, when the boy seeks a masculine identity he may go to the unrealistic extreme of being very tough and entirely nonsentimental. One way to be tough (and, to be sure, an obvious one) is to commit delinquent acts that are becoming to a man.

Cohen (9) subscribes to Parson's point of view about middle-class delinquency. He adds, "Good behavior is symbolized by (mother's) feminity, whereas 'bad' acts stand for masculinity; and a lad who grows up in a family dominated by feminine figures and images thus asserts his manhood by being 'bad', i.e., deviant." And Lemert (10) evolved his closure theory to explain the naive check forgeries of persons who are not financially needy. Subjectively-felt social isolation resolves itself in an act of impulsive forgery, leading to punishment of oneself or some relevant others.

In homosexuality, the self-concept is all important. The realization by the latent homosexual of his deviant tendencies, and the crystallization of his new identity—what is called "coming out"—clarifies uncertainties and disperses the diffusion in his self-concept (11). This is reportedly a pleasant, tension-releasing experience. On the other hand, a heterosexual self-concept, when enhanced by strict rules for behavior, remains intact even if a man engages regularly in male prostitution (12).

Probably the best illustration of the development of a deviant self-concept is the history of the thief-poet-philosopher, Jean Genet. Genet's self-image is one of a thief, an ex-con, a member of the criminal sub-culture. Although fact and fiction intermingle in his work, most of the events actually happened one way or another to Genet personally; so that his writing is a mixture of experience, feeling, and reminiscence.

Genet was born out of wedlock. His mother abandoned him in his cradle, and he spent his early formative years in the state orphanage in Paris. In due course he was entrusted to a foster-home, a peasant family in Le Morvan. At first he was happy, living the peaceful life of a village youngster; however, he soon realized that he was not like the other youngsters. He was a foundling, he had no mother, no father, and therefore he had no clear identity to internalize. The village was a closed community, and so was the peasant family. The other children in the family attributed any mishap or misdeed to "the little bastard" from the orphanage, and so Genet soon came to represent unwanted and despised attributes, both of the family and the small peasant community. His self-image, the inner anchor of his identity, consisted of these negative definitions, images, and characteristics, given to him by the relevant others. Genet did his utmost to comply with this negative image, and willfully, almost joyfully, plunged into depths of negativism. He finally knew who he was, for he had been given the self-image he had never had—as it happened, that of a pederast and a thief.

An outsider like Genet who complies with the images of evil imputed to him by the surrrounding others feels that by assuming the role he serves the group. By being evil, because he has been defined as evil, the outsider feels that he has fulfilled a mandate—he has submissively conformed, and society owes him, if not acclaim, at least acceptance. If he is not accepted, his disillusionment is bitter. Convicts who have been accused of committing a crime may, against all common prudence, be seized with an urge to confess, a wish to expiate themselves, to turn over a new leaf, to repay the theft—all in order to be reaccepted by one magic act of confession, of compliance, of redemption. Some confess even when the prosecution has scant evidence against them, and then feel lighthearted and at ease. It is as if they have said, "You, judge, jury, attorneys, the world at large, you say I am evil. All right, I am. But now we are quits. My confession means you have to accept me—you owe it to me." But rejection, not acceptance, is the inevitable result; and this is the essence of the outsider's dilemma.

Treachery, theft, and homosexuality are Genet's sacred trinity. He raises these three perverse elements to the rank of a theology (13) in opposition to the bourgeois virtues of loyalty, sanctity of private property, and heterosexuality. He also extols the straight-forward frankness of the criminal world over the hypocrisy and double standard of "your world."

To Genet, the act of crime means vigor, freedom, and fulfillment. Vigor, because the criminal puts a lot of energy and concentration into an act of stealing, it has a "terminal oneness," a combination of sacrifice and damnation which, for Genet, is the epitome of moral vigor (14). Freedom, because the commission of a crime or a betrayal gives one a sense of ease without any moral preoccupation, a feeling of expiatory detachment (15). Fulfillment, because the inner violence of the act of theft gives it a ritualistic and religious aura—it becomes an expiating sacrifice, an offering.

When Genet commits a crime, he acts according to the self-image imposed on him, and complies with the expectations of his immediate environment. This in itself is satisfying. The criminal Genet, with no parents and no past, with a precarious present and uncertain future, at last finds an identity that is his alone: nobody is going to challenge him for it, or take it away from him. Furthermore, complying with the image of a criminal not only gives him an identity, but also makes him eligible to enter the group of other thieves and homosexuals, thus giving him a group identity and a sense of belonging. Empirical confirmation of this explanation for criminal behavior was provided by Lewin, who showed that the emotional tension of adolescent youths was greatly diminished when they finally became members of a criminal gang, which gave them the identity they desired (16). The crucial point, however, is that every new act of crime then reinforces this identity, with a resultant feeling of accomplishment, elation, and vigor.

Value Deviation

The second component of our phenomenological model of deviance deals with detachment of value from the group's normative system—a detachment not necessarily accompanied by overt deviant behavior. I would like to use the sixteenth-century term, *accidia* or *accidie* to denote this detachment, in the same way that *anomy, anomie* and *anomia* are now used to denote normative disintegration in society.

For Durkheim *anomie* was a collective hangover caused by a social (mainly economic) shock. Its manifestations included the breakdown of controls over man's aspirations: "Whatever class has been especially favored by the disturbance [of affluence] is no longer disposed to its former self-restraint, and, as a repercussion, the sight of its enhanced fortune awakens in the groups below it every manner of covetousness. Thus the appetites of men, unrestrained now by a public opinion which has become bewildered and disorientated, no longer know where the bounds are before which they ought to come to a halt. . . . Because prosperity has increased, desires are inflamed. . . . The state of rulelessness or *anomie* is further heightened by the fact that human desires are less disciplined at the very moment when they would need a stronger discipline" (17). This statement relates exclusively to the normative rupture of society. The effect of anomie on individuals is taken for granted: the normative enclosure has burst open, the containment imposed by boundaries and limits has disintegrated, and the individuals are exposed to the disrupting effects of limitless desires and boundless aspirations.

Merton also stresses the societal nature of anomie, although in his classic exposition of *Social Structure and Anomie* (18) Merton expressly deals with individual modes of adaptations, including maladaptations. Merton's analysis, however, is based on the group, on the disjuncture between the social structure and the cultural system—that is, between social goals and the normative avenues to achieving them. Although individuals are affected by these social disjunctions, Merton's units of analysis are still societies and not individuals. He expressly excludes from his study mental processes which cannot be anchored in the social and cultural levels of analysis. According to Merton, "Anomie refers to a property of a social system. . . . Anomie, then, is a condition of the social surroundings, not a condition of particular people. . . to prevent conceptual confusion, different terms are required to distinguish between the anomie of individuals and the anomic state of the social system" (19). His concept of anomie is therefore focused on a societal state; the individual's confrontation with it is secondary, for Merton entirely disregards subjective states of mind.

Merton realized that his socially-focused conceptualization of anomie demanded a separate personal concept of anomie, for which he coined the word *anomia* (20). Accidia, however, denotes something more subjective than anomia. Merton implies that anomie, as a property of society, may be equated to the distribution of anomia as a property of individuals. But this is not a tenable position, since acute social anomie may not subjectively be perceived as such by individuals. The relationship Merton posits between anomie and anomia seems to be similar to the fallacious co-relation imputed by the Marxists to economic need as objectively measured in society and as subjectively conceived by individuals. The Marxists regard an objective state of economic need, as measured by a low standard of living, as a predisposing factor to crime and delinquency. Yet, an objective need such as starvation would not be regarded by most human beings as a sufficient justification for cannibalism, by Hindus as a sufficient incentive to slaughter sacred cows, or by orthodox Jews as a reason to eat pork. On the other hand, lack of enough money to buy a mink coat for a new mistress might be subjectively defined by some individuals as a need pressing enough to induce them to embezzle money from their employers.

Of the five types of alienation specified by Seeman (21), the first three—powerlessness, meaninglessness, and normlessness (anomie)—are clearly attributes of society, whereas the other two—isolation and self-estrangement—are subjective states of mind. However, they do not cover the same ground as value deviation. Powerlessness was the mode of alienation that Marx in his early writings imputed to capitalist society. He assumed it occurred when the worker does not have any means of control and decision over the processes of his work and its outcome. Later on, George Lukacs, the Marxist theoretician, used *fetishisation* to denote the estrangement of man's creations—when products have lost their normative or emotional meaning to the individual, so that he perceives them as a neutral dead weight on his mind (22). However, fetishisation still relates to the individual's surroundings; it is a condition of his environment and not of his subjective self.

The existentialist counterpart of the conceptualization of value deviation as a property of individuals is the idea that a person may become objectified to *himself*. It is like Sartre's estranged consciouslessness applied to the individual's self-image as perceived by himself. This objectification of the self as subjectively perceived by the individual is the core of my conceptualization of value deviation as an attribute of individuals and *not* of the social structure.

Accidia pertains to value deviation alone which may not have and need not have any overt behavioral manifestations. In medieval times, accidia was the fourth cardinal sin. It was the sin of not caring: "The fourth heed of the beast of hell is sloth, whych is callyd of clerkye accidye." It is characterized by heedlessness associated with depressive detachment, passivity, and sadness. As a state of mind, accidia has some resemblance to Camus' concept of the absurd as a *mood*. Camus' definition of the absurd is that "there can be no absurd outside of human mind" (23).

No doubt Marxists would condemn the idea that alienation is a subjective state of mind as an idealistic fallacy. However, Lukacs (24) described subjectivity as a self-contained entity, which struggles irrationally to express itself and is confronted with an alien and hostile reality.

Value deviation must naturally be considered in its cultural context. Because religious belief systems and ideologies are essentially based on value attachments, churches of every denomination have naturally been preoccupied with accida, sloth, and value detachment. All churches need to regain souls they consider lost, and to recapture strayed sheep; all have therefore evolved elaborate techniques of persuasion which in the Inquisition even extended to torture chambers. Other techniques, such as confession are used to reinforce the value attachment of the belief system by the self-condemnation of sins. It is therefore understandable that institutionalized religions have always been ambivalent toward mystical sects that preach value detachment, and tend to regard them as heretical.

The secular religions that sustain modern political ideologies display a similar fervor in condemning and persecuting value deviants. Their techniques of brainwashing are merely somewhat more sophisticated. Koestler's *Darkness at Noon* gave an insider's view of some of the techniques of treating value deviants in a totalitarian country, whereas Orwell's thought police seem to be a rather mild version of the ideological control system now operating in China.

Deviant Behavior

The third element in our scheme is actual deviant behavior. When the deviant individual himself is the object of his deviant acts, the deviation is *inwardly* directed. When the behavior is directed, as it generally is, toward the group and its social institutions, it is *out-*

wardly directed. We are presenting this dimension, in the following diagram, against the apparent motivation of the deviant behavior as it is manifested in the deviant acts themselves.

Inwardly Directed   **Outwardly Directed**

Autistic
    Self-Destructive
       Escapist
          Bohemian
            Accidental
              Acquisitive
                Rebellious

An extreme manifestation of inwardly-directed deviation is the *autistically alienated person.* Some of the advanced stages of schizophrenia are characterized by a complete breakdown of the individual's ties with reality; he may crouch in a corner and vegetate, or be gripped by hallucinations. Although the hallucinations may be associated with the individual's motor activity, their link with reality is slight.

The most apparent characteristic of schizophrenia is a person's withdrawal from reality, so that "thinking, feeling and action are no longer dominated by contact with other people or outside events, but are given over entirely to a world of fantasy whose only counterpart in the experience of normal people is the world of dreams" (25). Schizophrenia is characterized in its less severe forms by lack of ambition, apathy, withdrawal, and idleness. Acute cases are marked by prolonged stupor, immobility, complete disregard for surroundings; the sufferer is apparently totally absorbed in a "silent inner dream" (26).

A suicidal person is less removed from reality than someone who is autistic. The world to him is absurd, meaningless, tormenting, and unbearable; yet he has enough initiative to want to sever himself from it altogether, rather than withdraw into a dream.

Suicide, like autism, is extreme behavior. The group's reaction to suicide is generally extreme and rarely apathetic or indifferent. Albert Camus, both in *The Rebel* and *The Myth of Sisyphus,* says that the main ethical issue is whether a man's taking his own life is justified or not in given circumstances. Usually the group's attitude toward suicide or attempted suicide is derogatory and stigmatizing; sometimes, however, society places a hero's laurels on the suicide's grave.

Durkheim (27) noted that the real difference between what he called anomic and egoistic suicide, on the one hand, and altruistic suicide, on the other, is that society's attitudes are different toward these acts; it condemns anomic and approves of altruistic suicide. An anomic suicide may be stigmatized as a weakling, as many were who were driven to take their lives during the great depression of the early thirties. Egoistic suicide is the ultimate renunciation of social goals and norms, whereas an altruistic suicide—that of a hero who kills himself to save other lives, prevent a disaster, or win a battle—is the ultimate acceptance.

Robert Merton's premise (28) was that the retreat

of individuals from society and its norms occurs when some individuals fail to achieve social success goals by legitimate means, and yet have inner inhibitions against using illegitimate means to achieve these goals. The result is that they renounce both goals and means and become completely asocialized. Ohlin and Cloward (29) observed that the total rejection of social goals and the means of achieving them seen in retreatism may also be caused by the fact that barriers like racial prejudice may preclude the achievement of these goals. An alternative reason for retreatism is double-failure—where an individual has failed to achieve some goal by legitimate means, then resorts to illegitimate means, and fails there, too.

Other factors that also predispose a person to retreatism were described by Dynes, Clarke, and Dinitz (30). They found that burning ambitions and high aspirations represent an anxious quest for security by people with an unhappy childhood and unsatisfactory family relationships. Those whose early family relationships were satisfactory sought security in personal happiness and inner satisfaction, rather than in ambitious personal achievement; but when anxiety-ridden socialization and conflict within the family unit occur during an individual's formative years, it may result in a tendency to generalize negatively and to blame the whole of society for particular failures, thus preparing the ground for the rejection of social goals (31).

Presumably there is more retreatism in modern society than in earlier times, because there are fewer socially-approved places to retreat to. Individuals in modern society are more and more expected to exhibit a "radar-like sensitivity to how one is navigating in the social world, and the tendency to make that navigation into an end of life as well as a means" (32). The more individualistic inner-directed personalities are therefore more likely to be seen as marginal, because they do not conform to the prevailing trend of joyful adjustment to the expectations of others.

The intellectuals and artists who are dedicated to the expression and formulation of feelings and ideals in words, plastic arts, or other creative areas are very often detached from and indifferent to the prevailing norms and values of the society they live in. Their creativity and methods of operation do not permit them to get involved in the rat race for power, social status, and wealth. In order to deepen his insight and observation, the bohemian divorces himself from social realities; thus he gains the necessary distance and perspective to observe and analyze these same realities.

The essence of the bohemian deviation is a physical and moral detachment from the group: a different way of looking at things, and a different hierarchy of values. Paradoxically, bohemians always aesthetically express and intellectually expound the existence, goals, and ideals of the group; they are able to do this simply because they are spectators. The bohemian deviation was once described by Montesquieu (33): "That which shocked me most is that they are quite useless to their country and amuse their talents with puerilities. For example, when I arrived at Paris, I found them warm at dispute over the most trifling matter imaginable. It was all about an old Greek poet."

Bohemians may sometimes be the nucleus of a sub-culture, but very often this cafe society degenerates into a pseudo-bohemia. Pseudo-bohemian groups of a very few real artists, surrounded by a multitude of self-styled artists, perpetual would-be artists, and camp followers are an integral part of society—an institutionalized layer of the social stratification—and are accepted as such by the other strata of society. Pseudo-bohemians are therefore integrated in the social structure. The sign of genuine bohemia—a disregard for all goals that are not aesthetic or artistic—does not exist in the prosperous cafe society; instead it includes people who conform exactly to the middle-class concept and image of the bohemian outsider, as expressed in dress, mannerisms, and demeanor.

A person may commit certain acts which are clearly deviant but not really intentional or persistent; for example, short-lived escapades to hide out, or involvement with alcohol, drugs, or women. These acts are committed by most people a few times in their lives and for relatively short periods. A very important factor is whether the accidental deviation is detected, or passes unnoticed, because discovery may well mean that it develops into a persistent pattern. Many youngsters indulge in occasional escapades of petty theft, violence, and forbidden pleasure ranging from stealing a boat or a car for a joy ride, through theft of money from parents or relatives. And adult conformists, too, from time to time indulge in a binge, become involved in illicit transactions, or temporarily embrace some "radical" ideas. If not exposed and stigmatized, these temporary deviations generally do not affect a later election to the presidency of the local Rotary Club.

There are an increasing number of rebels without a cause today—hordes of aggressive teenagers and young adults who vent their rage, negativism, and aggression in chaotic rebellion. The values and norms of society are rejected and attacked, but the aims of and the motivations for the rejection are either confused or nonexistent. These violent teenagers are very often organized into gangs; they have their own norms and ways of acting, their special clothes and mannerisms; but these are mainly matters of form, rather than being goal-directed.

Many studies have described negativistic aggression, the seemingly purposeless vandalism that is part of this kind of delinquent behavior. One explanation for this rebellion without a cause (34) ascribes it to the insecurity of youths who first halfheartedly infringe middle-class norms, and who then, in order to overcome their guilt feelings, react with exaggerated bravado and aggression against subconsciously cherished middle-class standards. However, this overt aggression may be not so much a reaction formation as a direct and positive rebellious act, a battle-cry against double thinking, double talking, and the clearly contradictory and confused value systems of socializing agencies—families, schools, churches, and other social institutions.

Maturity is the ability to reconcile the contradictory postulates of culture, and to develop a selective attitude toward various groups. Adolescence, on the other hand, is characterized by a yearning for absolute values and a desire for sharply defined roles. Youth has always been a time for idealism; it is also a time for passionate desire for consistency and honesty. The chaotic rebel may be unable or unwilling to accept the basic hypocrisies of our society or to use double standards. As a result, modern educators and socializing agencies see to it that any such manifestations of spontaneity and individuality are suppressed very early, in order to prevent the catastrophes of immaturity and maladjustment.

The rebel with an ideology wishes to overthrow governments, and change social, economic, and religious institutions. He is motivated by his faith that when his ideologies or goals govern the fate of the group, there will be a clear road to equality, justice, power, revolution, peace, and utopia.

However, utopia is an unattainable vision, and on the endless road that leads to it, most rebels, social reformers, political innovators, and founders of religious succumb, either intentionally or not, to the pursuit of power. Political and bureaucratic control becomes the main goal; and though social control may or may not help to achieve The Cause, it is certainly instrumental in preserving the position of the power elite.

Social Stigma

The fourth component in our phenomenological scheme is social stigma. Stigma here means a derogatory attribute imputed to the social image of an individual or group, and used as a tool of social control.

As such, we may analyze the link between social stigma and crime and deviation on two levels: first, what effect social stigma has on the initial recruitment of an individual into crime and deviation; and second, its effect on further crime and deviation after a person has once run afoul of the machinery of law enforcement and other mechanisms of social control. This second aspect of social stigma is related to its formal effects. The stigma of having been convicted a criminal, or of having been identified and tagged as a deviant limits a person's socioeconomic opportunities and forcibly changes his status and role. At first he may merely reject some of the legitimate group's norms, and seek the company of other ex-convicts and deviants, but eventually a total rejection of the norms and values of the legitimate group may lead to the adoption of the normative system of the deviant group.

The most notable contribution to the theoretical analysis of the effects of stigma on deviance is Tannenbaum's now classic description of how society tags and isolates the delinquent group (35). Howard Becker examined the effect of stigma on the self-concept of individuals who joined deviant groups—for instance, marihuana users and dance musicians. Cloward and Ohlin (36) used social stigma to explain the formation of deviant juvenile groups:

> The initial contrast between the individual and the authorities over the legitimacy of certain social norms

and the appropriateness of certain acts of deviance sets in motion a process of definition that marks the offender as different from law-abiding folk. His acts and his person are defined as "evil" and he is caught up in a vicious cycle of norm-violation. The process of alienation is accelerated, and the chasm between the deviant and those who try to control and reform him grows wider and deeper. In such circumstances the delinquent subculture and the prevailing bases of an individual's rejection becomes increasingly dependent on the support of others in his position. The gang of peers forms a new social world in which the legitimacy of delinquent conduct is strongly reinforced.

Genet's description remains the most telling. He sees himself as a scapegoat, as a receptacle of abuse, refuse, and vileness. In these circumstances, every additional negation is a triumph, and being a criminal is a worthy sacrifice. This salvation does not only belong to Genet himself, but serves as a sort of cleansing mechanism for the pollution of others. He is the scapegoat, the damned. All the evils that the community casts off are transferred symbolically to him. By accepting these symbolic stigmatizing stones, he is ritually expiated, and he cleanses the others of their sins by taking them upon himself. This is the reason he claims ritualistic fulfillment—the beatitude of a thief. However, there is no hopeful resurrection for him; he has learned that when he vicariously expiates the evil of others through behaving as scapegoat, he will never be paid with social acceptance in this world or with heavenly love in the everafter.

Our view of social stigma synchronizes two casual

levels. The first is an assortment of predisposing factors, the second a chain of dynamic processes that leads to the actual stigmatization. The predisposing factors are those forms of value deviation and deviant behavior which in a given culture raise the probability that an individual will be stigmatized. I stress the cultural element, because these predisposing factors vary from one society to the other. It is also possible, however, that an individual may be stigmatized as deviant although he is a conformist both in his values and behavior.

I shall analyze the dynamic processes of stigma by first tracing its psychological origins, then considering the socio-psychological factors involved in the relationship of the individual to his group, and finally examining the meaning and nature of stigma as a social act of power.

Inner aggression and the projection of guilt for the stigmatizer's own deviant tendencies are the subconscious sources of the social stigma. The urge to stigmatize is presumably linked to an individual's own aggression, and to the free-floating aggression of groups. Inner negativity and group tension find at least partial release in the derogatory branding of others. Social stigma is thus an institutionalized safety valve, and similar in function to the Roman circuses, to bullfights, public hangings, and wrestling and boxing matches. The mechanism of projection as a psychological source of stigma has been described by Flugel (37) as follows: People "experience delight in gossip and scandal in which they gloat over the pecadillos and frailties of their neighbors and acquaintances. They are indulging their own guilty desires vicariously, preserving their own virtue intact (the implication is that they themselves would never partake in such scandalous proceedings as those under discussion) and expressing their disapproval through appropriate inflections of the voice and shaking of the head."

The release of frustrations and resentment through the subconscious mechanisms of transference and scapegoating also serves as the catalyst for the psychic formation of a social stigma, which is then applied against a specific individual or group.

The choice of the objects of a social stigma is governed by conspicuous differences which arouse fear and anxiety in the stigmatizer. The choice of the objects is also determined by their relative powerlessness and hence vulnerability to stigma. The stigmatized are very often chosen in a rational and formalized manner, as in illegal behavior. In other cases, although the choice is ir-rational and subconscious, it is not random. A major factor determining the choice is that the objects are different in a symbolically relevant way, and therefore disturbing or menacing.

From ancient times, the members of out-groups have been considered not only different but actually dangerous, not potential but real enemies (38). In ancient Greece, for instance, where policy-making was quite realistic, stigmatization by ostracism—described as "clipping off the tallest ears of corn" (39)—meant concentrating on those who seemed to be more conspicuous than necessary. The question for the assembly was: "Is there any man among you who you think is dangerous to the State? If so, who?" In other words, conspicuousness was equated with danger. Difference implies menace, and the most obvious, those who were most different, were stigmatized.

Social stigma in an achievement-obsessed culture may serve as an illusory achievement for those who have failed at real achievement. Because achievement is relative, an individual can "achieve" by branding others derogatorily. When an individual or group that craves success as compensation for insecurity and anxiety does not achieve these goals, they will try to achieve status by lowering the status of the stigmatized. This is the actual function of stigma; it is as recognizable in the man who belittles a rival as it is in the perennial inclination of the socially insecure lower middle-class to hate out-groups, Jews, and members of other races.

Stigma applied to a successful innovation can explain away the inventor's performance so as to narrow the gap between the stigmatizer and the stigmatized: if I cannot be as good as John Smith, I can at least neutralize his success by bringing it down to my level. The Nazis, for instance, stressed that Germany did not actually lose World War I. "It was not they, the celestial Teutons, who had lost the war, it was the Jews and the Marxists who slyly and surreptitiously had administered the fatal stab in the back which made them reel and falter" (40). It was not a fair fight. However, no logical or material link need be apparent between the stigma and the superiority of the stigmatized. Usually the connection is superfluous or non-existent. Cause and effect seem to be irrelevant for explaining away success by means of stigma.

The stigma of maladjustment is acquired in a way similar to the stigma of a criminal. It is linked neither to ethics, metaphysics, nor justice, but to an act of power directed against an individual or a group too conspicuously different, whose existence or behavior is detrimental to the powerful stigmatizing agencies. The essence of social stigma on the social level is embodied in Inez Cirano's statement to Garcin in Sartre's *No Exit:* "You are a coward, Garcin, because I want it to be so." The Roman *infamia* is an excellent illustration of stigma used as an act of power. The criteria for this declaration were so amorphous as to amount to complete freedom for the censor to brand any person he chose with the stigma of *infamia* (41).

Sumners' description (42) of the normative basis of social mores fits the conception of stigma as a social act.

Nothing but might has ever made right. If a thing has been done and is established by force, it is right in the only sense we know, and rights will follow from it which are not vitiated at all by the force in it. We find men and parties protesting, declaiming, complaining of what is done and which they say is not "right." They lose sight of the fact that disputes always end in force. Therefore, might has made all the right which ever has existed or exists now. The habit of using jural concepts, which is now so characteristic of our mores, leads us into vague and impossible dreams of social affairs, in which metaphysical concepts are supposed to realize themselves, or are assumed to be real.

Pressure, coercion, and stigma are applied by the group (or by individuals who possess enough power to do so) when some interest or value of the group (or of a powerful individual) has been infringed on or injured. No other criterion has the same significance. Justice, ethics, piety, and positive values are at best only formal and idealized criteria for differentiating between the delinquent and the good, the misfits and the adjusted. The criterion which actually triggers the process of dividing the criminal and nonconformist from the law-abiding and conforming population is the power element of social stigmatizing. Nothing else could define the mythical crime of Prometheus and the antisocial behavior of Socrates, Alcibiades, Savonarola, and Jesus Christ: they acted against the interests of groups which had enough power to ostracize them and ultimately to exterminate them.

In the last analysis, a criminal, a deviant, or an antisocial person is one who is branded and treated as such by a group or an individual with the power to do so. The mark of Cain is mainly an exercise of power by the branders who are able to put tags on individuals or groups who don't fit in. As far as crime is concerned, there are certain legal limits to social branding; but there are no barriers to stigmatizing a person as deviant or maladjusted. The criteria for doing so are necessarily vague, and change with every shift in the power structure of government, or with developments in custom and other components of the social system. Once started, the effects of stigma are powerful. The pressure exerted by segregation and stigmatizing is all downward and the way back up to higher social status is blocked by many barriers. Kafka's K. insisted on his innocence, but social stigma by itself was more than enough to establish his guilt.

This potency of social stigma has induced many social scientists, notably Becker (43) and Goffman (44), to redefine deviance in terms not of the act or the actor, but of the labels with which these acts and actors have been tagged.

Deviance and Transcendence

The last element in our model deals with the transcendental aspects of deviance. The idea of salvation through sin is essentially the maxim that negation is sacred. The more extreme the negation, the greater the chances of salvation—so long as one is kindled by faith. If laws and morals are in conflict with faith, faith prevails. Johannes Agricola, the antinomian preacher, commanded: "Art thou steeped in sin, an adulterer or a thief? If thou believest, thou art in salvation. All who follow Moses must go to the Devil. To the Gallows with Moses."

One aspect of this theme of salvation through the gutter is the story of the descent of Jesus into Hell in order to save some worthy fallen souls. Thomas Mann (45) retells another similar legend—that one of the popes of Christendom, born of an incestuous union between a brother and sister, later sired children by his own mother. This sinner, Gregorius, was chosen to be Vicar of Christ *because* of his sins, which made him suitable for beatitude. "A child of shame, his mother's spouse, his grandfather's son-in-law, his father's father-in-law, monstrous brother of his own children, was led to St. Peter's seat." Sin, thus, is a prerequisite of salvation. Mann portrays in this story not only the dialectical interchange of purity and pollution, but the instrumentality of sin in opening the door of Paradise.

According to Hindu doctrine (46) perfection is achieved by satisfying all desires—including theft, sexual perversion, and cannibalism. The focus here is on perfection, perfect evil being at the opposite pole, but on the same line, as perfect good. For those who understand that both evil and good are illusory and that true reality is beyond good and bad, all immorality and the infringement of any law are permitted. Many other justifications for the doctrine of beatitude through sin have been offered by the Jewish Kabbalists and heretical messianic sects. The Kabbalah allocates to great souls the task of delving into sin and pollution in order to raise particles of purity, because lesser souls would not have the power to lift themselves up again from the evil swamps (47).

Great esteem for penitents has also been used to justify the sacred sin that leads to salvation, to unification with God. The Talmud's assertion that the penitent is worthier than the one who never sinned has been interpreted by some sects as a mandate to infringe laws and morals in order to be able to achieve greater sanctity. Jacob Frank, the Jewish apostate Messiah, visualized Jacob's ladder in the shape of a V (48), a symbol of the idea that before one ascends to Divinity, one has to fall from grace. The road to Heaven is through Hell. Frank interpreted the passage from Genesis: "Get thee out of thy country and from thy kindred unto a land that I will show thee" as meaning that Jews should join the Edomites, the children of Esau, the Christians. From this intentional blasphemy, which is the ultimate sin, the road can lead only up to a new salvation. Frank made good his antinomian promise to his followers to "break all laws" by starting with his own family and taking his daughter as his mistress. Frank also had an apocalyptic vision: everything was to be destroyed; amidst disaster, he would lead his followers into depravity and perdition, because their evil world was created by an evil God and by destroying his commandments, they would pave the way for the perfect unblemished God.

The conspiratorial secrecy of the Frankists was also due to their efforts to reverse all temporal being. Things should not be as they *appear* to be, and all appearances must be diametrically opposed to the core of things. The basis for this idea was a mystical text describing the

Saviour King as the purest of the pure, dressed in vile garments. They interpreted this to mean that the outwardly evil appearance of an act disguises its inner virtue, and these evil outward qualities are directly proportional to the secret inner goodness which they represent. By the same token, the severity of the infringement of a norm represents a symmetrically opposite virtue. That is the meaning of the paradoxical maxim of the Frankists, that "to abolish the Torah is to uphold it" (49). Frank even proclaimed that those who talk and act the way they really feel and think are not true believers. The sacred task of self-salvation must always be secret and disguised (50). The routine of temporal life should go on while underneath the search for salvation continues secretly and in silence. The Frankists were certainly quite sincere in their messianic beliefs. Their aim was nothing less than salvation through the gutter. Frank himself paid for his convictions when the Polish priests decided that his conversion to Catholicism was just a facade for his heresy, and imprisoned him in the Chenstochov fortress (51).

Although sex has lost most of its hedonistic mystique, those who regard existence as evil continue to attack it as the source of all that is bad. The Zervanties of ancient Persia, gloomy worshippers of an evil Ahriman who dominated an evil temporal creation, regarded Az, sexual desire, and Jeh, the woman-whore, as the main pillars of Ahriman's reign (52). The Buddha fights Kama, sexual pleasure, because it "is the seducer of men, for through pleasure men are reborn and so chained to the wheel of existence" (53). The same view was expressed by the Kabbalists, who equated evil with temptation and sex.

The sexual excesses of de Sade were an assault on mores, laws, and ethics, a stride toward the goal of anarchy. Genet and Frank, on the other hand, preach antisex, either the perversion or the humiliation of the procreative act. Luis Bunuel ends his film *The Milky Way (La Voie Lactee)* with the following episode: two tramps, who have crossed all of Spain in a pilgrimage to the tomb of St. James of Compostella, find out that the man who was actually buried in the tomb was Prisilian the Apostate. Prisilian preached that the body should be humiliated by adultery and lechery in order to achieve purity—that is, salvation through the defilement of sex.

A Yogi or a Buddhist monk may spin around in a circular unity, whirling incessantly on the circumference of a Mandala with no beginning and no end, where good and bad are just empty labels. Rabbis and bishops, on the other hand, are more inclined by cultural heritage to define, judge, and condemn; they must have a bad to contrast with a good. Moreover, they must maintain a delicate balance between dualism, which is downright heresy, and monism, which cannot be defined by contrast. The dialectic swing of the pendulum is therefore God's best gift to His institutionalized followers. We are the holy and pure; our sanctity is affirmed by contrast with polluted sinners; and the synthesis is achieved through their punishment and repentance, and by our granting of grace, pardon, and expiation.

A case in point is the compromise that Zervan afforded between good and evil in Zoroastrianism. Zervan the Father, like Mitra the Mediator, provided the balance between two conflicting divine entities. In like manner, Satan and the Sitra-Achra have always been held in check by the Godhead in institutionalized Judaeo-Christianity. Some of the Kabbalists have suggested that the cosmic catastrophe of the "Breaking of the Vessels," which is equated with human birth, was engineered by God in order to create evil so that good would be defined by exclusion and contrast (54).

To Jung, the anti-Christ is a dark complementary mirror image of Christ; together Christ and the anti-Christ make up the unity of the Self (55). Saint Paul postulates the contrasting function of evil, when he says: "I find then a law, that, when I would do good, evil is present with me." Evil becomes a necessity. Without it, the image of Christ, the good self, remains blurred. The contrasting of evil gives the Savior substance and body—a point well symbolized by His crucifixion between two thieves.

Jung considers Christ the symbol of the suffering self (56). By instinct, for survival and sanity, each of us is at odds with all the other human beings, and must favor ourselves over all the others. But every one of these others also elevates himself above the rest, so that each of us inevitably must be hurt when others do not evaluate our uniqueness as we do. One way to deal with this is to regard oneself as a suffering Christ. But for Christ to be crucified, he needs a Judas to betray him;

and so the image of salvation is always linked with betrayal. The function of the deviant is to define the contour of the conformist just as the sinner defines the contour of the saint. Judas was crucial to Christ; indeed, he has even been portrayed as the greater saint by the Iscariots. Judas did not wish to be Judas, he performed his treason as a sacrifice and as a sacred duty. The sinister path to salvation has at times been glorified even by institutionalized clerics. Scholem (57) tells us of a Talmudic scholar who would infringe some of the most solemn rules in order to be cleansed afterward by the pangs of repentance. And Frank's sacred mission was to betray God in order to expedite the coming of the Savior (58).

Religion has always equated crime with sin, because their illegal or nonconforming behavior angers the Gods. Since a sinner-deviant irritated the deities, his presence in a community meant danger. Gods are likely to pour their wrath on the whole community, rather than only on the one at fault. Deviants were polluted and pollution may spread; consequently, punishment cleansed not only the deviant, but the whole community. To purify, to cleanse, to expiate, one has to punish the sinner whose sin, therefore, is a prerequisite for salvation. Some Indian sects, part of the cult of Siva, took the sanctity of pollution literally. They ate corpses and all kinds of excrement; their food was served in cups and dishes fashioned from human skulls (59).

The Kabbalists regarded mercy as the "right hand of God" and the source of goodness; His wrath emanates from His left hand, which is also the source of evil (60). That is to say, Divine wrath (and righteous indignation of man) creates the polluted (sinners), the damned (deviants), and the evil (criminals), and God first makes sinners with His stern judgment in order to be able afterward to save them. Christ descended into Hell to save some worthy souls—for true holiness is achieved as a sequel to pollution.

The black furies would pursue any
planet that should wander out of its orbit.

ANAXAGORAS

CHAPTER **IV**

THE

QUEST

FOR

STABILITY

A functional analysis of deviance, unlike the phenomenological one, presupposes a certain inherent order and purpose in the social structure; a system in balance with elaborate rules of equilibrium. Durkheim's and Parsons' models are based on the presumption that there is a tendency for human beings, both as individuals and as members of groups, to reach a congruous state of mind. They also imply that a state of stability, harmony, and adjustment is the "good" state of affairs. This line of thought, presupposing the central unity of things, runs from the pre-Socratic philosophers, through Plato's equation of justice with order, to some contemporary psychiatrists who regard the balanced personality as a desirable goal. To those who argue that these assumptions are simplistic, one may answer with Cioran's words (1): "Men's minds need a simple truth, an answer which delivers them from their questions, a gospel, a tomb. The moment of refinement conceals a death-principle. Nothing is more fragile than subtlety." Consequently, any disruption of this balance, every pressure away from the desired state of functional equilibrium is interpreted as deviance.

Our functional analysis of deviance will run as follows: 1) Movement away from or the infringement of an ideal norm which is set from above; 2) Divergence from the mean, median, or modal behavior in groups; 3) Change or disruption in the stable state of a social structure.

The Ideal Norm

Platonic ideal behavior is often imposed by rule setters as a goal which may not necessarily be achieved. The rationale behind the excessive demands of an ascetic rabbi or the puritanical prudishness of a New England preacher is that holding up a very remote saintly ideal may make the people in their congregations lesser sinners. Ideal norms are advocated not because of any belief in the possibility of their attainment, but as an absolute to strive and long for. Consequently, deviance is measured by how much individuals and groups fall short of this absolute ideal. The fact that many, or even most, of the individuals in a given group do not meet this ideal norm—that is, they are deviants—is irrelevant. Conformity and deviance are measured not by comparing the position of an individual in relation to the modal behavior of the group, but in relation to an abstract rule, law, or dogma.

There is a difference between falling short of an ideal norm, and violating a criminal law which remains binding even though not every one observes it. So many Americans gamble, for instance, that one sometimes gets the impression that organized crime is an American way of life (2). Nonetheless, gamblers are still deviants, because the criterion here is the binding rule (criminal law), and not the modal behavior of individuals.

Most of the rules that set purposely high ideals while disregarding the possibility of their achievement have to do with morals and religion. Some Protestant theologians regard the essence of transcendental belief as the longing for the achievement of an absolute which is unattainable by definition, while others regard human longing itself as the essence of the religious experience. Eastern religions advocate an ideal annihilation of the self—a goal that is very rarely reached. In the realm of morals, Camus points out that Sisyphus is right precisely because his task cannot be accomplished. On a much lower level, fashions also represent ideal goals for the public. High-style clothes, male and female beauty as personified in movie idols—all are ideal models as remote and unattainable as perfect goodness.

On the group level, there is Durkheim's virtual beatification of solidarity. The group, society, the state are the ideal; everything which falls short of total devotion to the group is deviance. Here, too, deviance is virtually inevitable, because the higher the group's idealized expectations for individuals, the higher the rate and severity of deviance (3). However, Durkheim's group ideal is moderate compared to other blueprints for Utopias, from those of Charles Faurier and Tommasco Companella to the more imposing states of Plato and Karl Marx. All these assume that the masses and the working classes do not really know what is good for them, and the Olympian philospher-kings and the dictators of the proletariat have to continually point out what is right. These ultimate ideals are then broken down into detailed intermediate goals, which allows for an operational definition of deviants: those who did not reach the daily quota of sparrow killing, those who could not grow enough corn in time for the inspection of the Komissar, or those who were responsible for the failure of five-year plans to produce more consumer goods than Japan. The number of deviants is irrelevant, because for the militant utopian the ideal norm is the only measure of conformance. Because this norm cannot be questioned, deviants are those who do not reach it, regardless of their efforts. In the inevitably authoritarian vocabulary of Utopia there are no justified failures (4).

Nothing in Excess

The work by Svend Ranulf on the ancient Greek value systems (5) indicates the importance of the golden mean. The Greeks believed each person has his *moira* (his predetermined fate in life); if he exceeds it by being conspicuous in any way—too wealthy, too successful or too wise—he is guilty of hubris, and arouses the jealousy of the gods. Tragic heroes like Tantalus, Polycrates, Prometheus, and Sisyphus all owe their plight to a spectacular success or a colossal failure. Prometheus, for instance, was punished not because he brought fire to humanity, but because his knowledge of architecture, astronomy, mathematics, medicine, navigation, and metallurgy made Zeus angry. Prometheus was different (and therefore dangerous) in many ways. Tantalus was another innovator, who was punished for proving that the sun is a mass of white-hot metal.

Herodotus recounts the message of Artabanos to Xerxes: "You see that God hurls his bolt against those living beings that tower above the rest. He does not suffer them to exalt themselves. The small ones on the other hand do not bother him. You see that the lightning always strikes the tallest houses and trees. For God loves to set a limit to everything that rises too high. For God does not suffer anyone but himself to harbor proud thoughts."

Agamemnon's hubris lay in his allowing the Greeks to hail him as the "highest of all who walk on earth today." But, as Aeschylus writes, "The black furies wait, and when man has grown by luck, not justice, great with overturn of chance, they wear him to a shade; and cast down to perdition, who shall save him?"

Modesty and the golden mean are also two of the cornerstones of Judaic ethics. The image of spiritual greatness has always been associated with self-deprecation. "Don't be modest, you are not yet great," a sage admonished his students. And Job was afflicted because he pridefully *felt* righteous—that is, he was guilty of hubris.

Condemning someone for being conspicuous means condemning him for being strange, and therefore dangerous (6). The Azande in Africa ostracize as witches persons who are deformed, ill-tempered, glum, or behave bizarrely—all signs of their potential danger (7). The heretics persecuted by the Inquisition were often merely those whose way of life, peculiarities of conversation, dress, manners, or conduct did not conform (8).

The universal appeal of the golden mean on the psychological level lies in the fact that it is based on the process of human decision-making. The perception of our senses and the consensus of others are the raw materials for our decisions; however, when the senses of an individual have been experimentally confronted with the contradictory consensus of some relevant others, he tends to conform with the consensus of the group (9). Apparently the tendency to follow the group, to adopt the view of the majority as determined by measures of modality and means, is a psychological characteristic of the human animal. The consensus of the majority reduces ego's anxiety, so that he has a sense of well-being and a feeling of security.

Central measures dominate both the psyche of the human individual and the organization of human groups. No wonder that the mode, mean, and median are the prime measuring rods for conformity and deviance.

Our present statistical conception of deviance is that it is the infringement of the modal values and behavior of a given group at a given time. Deviance varies, of course, with the shifting of the modes, means, and medians. Moreover, there can be no *a priori* definition of deviance from group modes because behavior which may be deviant in one situation can become modal in another. Merton's typology of adaptations (10), for instance, lists "ritualism" as an individual's anchorage in routine. The modal types in our industrialized and bureaucratized societies are ritualists—assembly-line technicians and clerks. Therefore, industrial psychologists as well as Chinese thought reform councils encourage these workers to identify their routine drudgery with a sacred aim, so that cultural goals are merged with the methods of achieving them.

Activity that shakes the foundation of a structure, or upsets a system's dynamic equilibrium is often defined as deviance. Conflict theorists, notably Simmel and Coser, however, see this kind of behavior as a dialectical movement toward social change and progress. These diametrically opposed points of view involve correspondingly divergent value judgments. Let us first consider the view of the "adjustment-centered" sociologists, who regard any disruption of the structure as dysfunctional—that is, bad for society and its institutions. Later on, we shall discuss the ideas of the conflict theorists, according to which the disrupture of a present equilibrium is just one phase in the dialectic movement toward a better state.

The idealization of stability is no doubt older than Plato, but he made a harmonious steadiness the underlying tenet of his social philosophy. He equated justice with co-operation and evil with the disruption of the social order. Other Western philosophers have also advocated the steady wholeness of the group and its normative system as a bulwark against social ills. Hegel had the traditional Teutonic reverence for the *status quo;* Comte praised social stability. Naturally, both of them staunchly advocated obedience and conformity to group norms. Hegel admired the Pythagorean notion of education, according to which a pupil must subordinate himself completely to his masters and elders for at least five years. Comte even thought the Indian caste system offered the best framework for social stability. The Spencerian notion of social progress was also anchored in stability: the lengthy process of growth through evolution necessitates a balanced social structure, because an abrupt disjuncture or a skewed change might result in a twisted and deformed growth. Tonnies thought his idealized *Gemeinschaft*—the cohesive concord of group numbers—generated more social stability than the purely normative conventions characteristic of the more diffuse *Gesellschaft*.

The most elaborate case for social stability was expounded by Durkheim, however (11). For him, the cohesive stability of the group was a necessary prior condition for the sanity of society and the well-being of its individuals. He even argued that human society affords the individual the only opportunity to become immortal by imprinting his ideas on the culture of the group. To fulfill its functions, a society should be cohesive, stable, and balanced and the individuals comprising it should give it their full support and solidarity. Consequently, the detachment of the individual from the group—that is, social deviance—is more likely when the group is disintegrated and its value system disrupted, or, to use Durkheim's own concept, when society suffers from anomie. Since suicide is the ultimate deviance —rejection of society—Durkheim tried to prove his point by comparing the suicide rates among Catholics, Protestants, and Jews. The rigidity of dogma and the hierarchical order of the Church produce greater social stability and therefore individual Catholics strongly identify with their groups. Jews, also, have a strong identification because they are rejected by other groups and in addition possess elaborate rituals which govern their lives. Both Catholics and Jews have lower suicide rates than Protestants, whose individualistic doctrine stresses personal responsibility toward God.

Other theorists in the social and behavioral sciences rely on the principle of homeostasis, which is the tendency of the human body to maintain steady states vital for its functions. The concept of a physiological homeostasis is extended and transferred to cognitive phenomena and to the perception of values and norms, and then used to define change or deviance in human behavior. Wynn-Edwards (12), for instance, in his work on the function of social norms relies heavily on his homeostatic theory of society, both animal and human.

He believes that natural selection has favored the evolution of man into a species that can transmit and adapt social values, so that he is free from the necessity of evolving entirely new ones with every change in the world around him. This new phase of social Darwinism makes conformity to new normative mandates necessary to the survival of man.

From this point of view, society preserves its homeostasis by defending itself against disruptive innovations and over-rapid social change. Cultural development, scientific discoveries, progress in the Spencerian sense, might be too sudden and too revolutionary if the pace of innovation were not curbed. Society has always had a built-in distrust and suspicion of all innovators, a defense that is reinforced by the low statistical incidence of real genius. Geniuses—genuine innovators—pay a price for their talent: they, too, usually meet rejection and dislike. This social homeostasis, however, does guard against too revolutionary and therefore disruptive innovations. Disproportionately rapid progress in any given area is likely to put it out of joint with other slower areas, and thereby cause disjunction. Very often previous achievement and knowledge may be too meager to support radical innovation and to absorb it into the social growth; or society may not be mature enough ethically to handle an innovation. Consequently, this homeostatic defense mechanism implies that innovation will be sacrificed to mediocrity, that consumption, production, and tastes will be standardized, and that all protrusions in the bureaucratic structure will be rounded off.

As Antonin Artaud has pointed out (13): "A lunatic is a man who preferred to become what is socially understood as mad rather than forfeit a certain superior idea of human honor. A vicious society has invented psychiatry to defend itself from the investigations of certain superior lucid minds whose intuitive powers were disturbing to it." The homeostasis of society operates, therefore, as a regulatory device, allowing a limited quantity and quality of innovations and innovators to survive, and destroying the rest.

The social deviance that disrupts the steady state of a group is anomie. Durkheim defined anomie as a state of "normlessness" in society, the antithesis of social solidarity; it is a state of ideological disintegration, of collective insecurity where the regulating forces of social norms have been impaired or destroyed altogether, and where no distinction can be made between the feasible and the impossible, between the just and the unjust.

The causes of social anomie are attributed by Durkheim mainly to sudden social change (14):

> When society is disturbed or disorganized, whether by a painful crisis or by a fortunate but too sudden turn of events, it is temporarily incapable of exercising normative control and influence on the individual.

Merton (15) also sees the state of anomie as a rupture, a dislocation, "a system of dissociation between culturally prescribed aspirations and socially structured avenues for realizing these aspirations."

Social change induced by the conflict of conduct

norms and other cultural mandates has also been linked to deviance. Sellin, one of the pioneers in the study of culture-conflict and deviance, says (16) : "Culture conflicts are sometimes regarded as by-products of a cultural growth process—the growth of civilization—sometimes as the result of the migration of conduct norms from one culture complex or area to another. However produced, they are sometimes studied as mental conflicts and sometimes as the clash of cultural codes." In criminological and social deviance research, culture-conflict has mainly been associated with social change and especially with immigration (17). Indeed, the clash of conduct norms caused by external and internal migration, and its links to crime and deviation, is more open to study than almost any other aspect of social change. As Sellin points out (18), culture-conflict encompasses a wide range of phenomena, from the dynamics of normative systems, on the social level, to norm conflicts as personality processes on the individual level (19).

Normative conflict situations presumably take place within the personality of the potential criminal or deviant before his first criminal acts or his initial recruitment into a deviant sub-culture. These internal conflicts and their subsequent first overt manifestations are crucial to the process by which a person comes to define himself, both to himself and to his relevant others, as delinquent and deviant. This is the transfer from the right side of the legal and social barricade to the wrong side. As he gradually is integrated more fully within the criminal or deviant group, with a corresponding rejection of the legitimate or square normative systems, he faces even more elaborate conflicts: narrowing of socioeconomic opportunities, rupture or jeopardizing of marriage and other domestic affiliations, mutual rejection of friends, as well as most of his former membership and reference groups. The last step is full-fledged membership in the criminal or deviant group. Essentially, therefore, he resolves his internal conflicts with life on the right side of the barricades by severing most of his relevant normative ties.

Some of the factors linked to conflicts in conduct norms are fluctuations in the rate of deviance; the appearance of special types of crime and deviance; urbanization; industrialization; internal and external migration; and the disintegration and secularization of traditional and tribal structures. Within this frame of reference there are factors that predispose to crime and deviance, among them anomalies in the structure of the family unit, economic factors, social change, social disorganization, and anomie. Culture-conflict may interact with all or some of these predisposing factors. The disintegration of immigrant family units by divorce, for instance, cannot be directly linked to the problems of adjusting to a new country. The disintegration of some families, on the other hand, is clearly due to the hardships imposed by clashes with the normative system of the absorbing country. Culture-conflict here, besides being a causal factor of delinquency in its own right because it is inherent to the social changes of migration, is also one of the causes of the disintegration of the family unit, which in turn is a classic factor in delinquency.

Economic hardship or affluence, as subjectively defined by an individual, can be related to culture-conflict and ultimately to crime and deviation if an individual's traditional self-image of economic sufficiency is shattered by the normative mandates of conspicuous consumption to which he is or becomes exposed.

The culture-conflict thesis, when applied to normative conflicts within the personality, may reveal some clues as to why one individual commits delinquent and deviant acts and another does not, and also explains why the individual has the attitude he does toward the restraining norm, and the degree to which he has internalized the restraining norm as a personality element. According to this point of view, norm conflict may affect delinquent behavior in two ways. First, conflict-situations may make the process of norm-sending ineffective, so that the norm is internalized by the individual at a very weak level or even not at all. And secondly, continuing conflicts in the norm-sending process may vitiate a set of norms already internalized. Under either of these circumstances, the normative barrier against a given crime or deviant act is completely shattered; the crime then lies in being caught and not in committing the offense.

Finally, we may note in relation to norm conflict that the criminal or deviant groups are part of the value systems of the prevailing culture. Some of the values of the criminal and deviant sub-culture may be tolerated by and be consistent with the values of the prevailing culture; and some may not. There are two norm and value ranges, then: one for the deviant group, and the other for the individuals who are associated with it. At one extreme we might find an ideal conformist, whose conflict with the prevailing normative system would be minimal. On the other extreme would be the individuals or groups who are totally opposed to the legitimate normative system. Such a completely negative group would be what Milton Yinger called a "contraculture": a subculture that is in normative opposition to the prevailing culture. An individual or group at a given time may range along this scale, depending on the amount and severity of how much conflict there is with the predominant normative system.

The law of causality, I believe, like much that passes muster among philosophers, is a relic of a bygone age, surviving, like the monarchy, only because it is erroneously supposed to do no harm.

BERTRAND RUSSELL
Mysticism and Logic

CHAPTER **V**

SOME

CAUSAL

INSIGHTS

Social deviance is too complex to have one cause or a single group of causes. Those explanations of deviance based on a single group of factors that had such a vogue in the nineteenth century, based on a belief in the omniscience of science, have faded away together with that century's other optimisms. In the behavioral and social sciences, elaborate complexities have replaced simplistic causal models. Today, multivariate analyses, expressed in probabilities and covariation, are the sophisticated and yet inexact tools that the student of deviance uses to discover significant links and relationships. Here, as in many other areas, the "denial of complexity," as Daniel Monaghan has said, "is a sign of tyranny." Or, in the words of Leslie Wilkins, who devoted much thought to the methodology of research in social deviance, "the causal processes which lead to deviance, can be discussed adequately only in terms of their complexity" (1).

The accepted way of presenting causal explanations

in the social sciences is to group conceptual systems, linked together by various modes of relationships, into models. However, causal model-making in social deviance is particularly difficult because much deviance is hidden. In criminology we must base any causal analysis on crimes known to the police; but these are not equally reported for the various types of offenses. Middle and upper class delinquency, for instance, is reported less than lower class delinquency.

The police know less about white collar crime than about other crimes committed by less privileged offenders. The victims of sexual assaults may choose not to complain to the police in order not to aggravate their suffering with publicity and police interrogations. Moreover, only a fraction—and in some types of offenses, notably property offenses, his fraction is rather small—of the people who commit crimes are detected and apprehended.

Identifying the extent and severity of deviant behavior is an even greater problem. Cohen (2) reports on the Russian institution of *Krugovaya poruka,* which has, no doubt, its equivalent in other societies. This is an express or tacit agreement by members within organizations, especially factories, to cover up reciprocally for deviant behavior, so that deviant acts are never identified as such by the authorities. If, for instance, a basic mistake in design has produced molds which are faulty, the designer knows that he can rely on the production engineer to "explain" the fault by some logical explanation. The director of the plant will accept this explanation because he is dependent on the designer and production engineer to cover up for *his* past and future mistakes. This circle of solidarity may sometimes involve many administrators in more than one organization.

The effect of the hidden crimes and unreported and unrecorded cases of deviance is to produce rates of criminality and deviance which do not adequately represent the whole population of criminals and deviants in a given society. Consequently, causal inferences about the personalities and processes which lead to deviance are based on faulty samples; and students of social deviance must keep this fact in mind whenever they evaluate a causal model of social deviance.

A Causal Model

Our causal model of deviance here will take into account: personality—some types of deviance are more likely to develop in conjunction with a particular stage of development; social factors—those present in a given society that raises the probability that a given individual becomes deviant; and dynamic processes that interact with the latent deviant tendencies of the individual and the social factors to release overtly deviant behavior.

Personality Factors of Deviance

The developmental stages which result in, first, the

crystallization of a separate ego and an ego-boundary, and later the appearance of an ethical ego identity, both involve us in pressures that must be overcome. The various demands of the mother and the relevant others, before the crystallization of the ego-boundary and after it, are perceived as disquieting events that we must cope and compromise with. Later on, we experience the demand that we fit into the boundaries of the normative system and evolve our own ego identity as another kind of developmental pressure.

These pressures may provoke deviant rather than conforming behavior if other conditions are right for it. A malformed ego boundary may be expressed as insanity and autistic schizophrenia, for instance. Or, a deviant neutralization of the ego identity may lead to crime and other modes of social deviance.

Particular types of deviance may manifest themselves at these stages of personality development, which may be directed inwardly or outwardly—that is, inside the ego boundary or outside. Transcendentally-based deviance, for example, may range from the mystic's inward efforts to annihilate the self to the heretic's outward rebellion against institutionalized religion.

One of the esoteric modes of mystical experience is the *mystical union*—the effacement of the self, the obliteration of the existence of the individual as a separate entity. The Kabbalists called this process *Iyun,* which means "becoming into nothingness." By this achievement of nonbeing, one annihilates the horrid attributes of separate existence, including death. The

Hindu *sadhana* also involves the dissolution of temporal existence "until everything is reabsorbed into the Great Brahma" (3). This death of the separate self gains eternal life through participation in unity.

The essence of Iyun—self-annihilation—has been described as follows (4):

> Every day we mention the redemption from Egypt, for by means of these letters we can unite our inner life force to God; but first we have to detach our life force from material thoughts and from the being of ourselves in order to enter the gate of Nothingness. Then we shall easily cleave with our roots into the cause of all causes. This is the meaning of the redemption from Egypt.

Many modes of mystical union have been sanctioned by the religious establishment throughout the ages. Nirvana and Samadhi, for instance, are the essence of major Far-Eastern religions; however, the mode of mystical union involves only the individual who seeks union. There are, on the other hand, some modes of institutionalized religious behavior that focus on the group and operate through the ecclesia. In these modes the mystical element is rather less important than rituals which are essentially magical. Indeed, a mystic who actively participates in a religious power structure is bound to become less mystical.

The acceptance of a mystic within the structure of institutionalized religion can be precarious; very often he is considered deviant. Molinos, the Christian mystic, was proclaimed the "personification of the quietist heresy" (5); the Maggid of Mezeritsch, on the other hand, who preached similar doctrines of annihilation of the self and union with divinity through quietism, was the leader of a very influential Chassidic movement.

The extreme religious deviants are the heretics and the satanists. Institutionalized religion has always been and still is one of the most forceful mechanisms for normative control. Logic is unnecessary, and normative gaps are bridged over by decrees supported by a metaphysical hierarchy.

Freud (6) pointed out the disharmonies which are presumably glossed over by institutionalized religion: "For the individual, as for mankind in general, life is hard to endure. Man's seriously menaced self-esteem craves for consolation, life and the universe must be rid of their terrors, and incidentally Man's curiosity . . . perhaps indeed we are not even defenseless, we can have recourse to the same methods against these violent supermen of the beyond that we make use of in our community: we can try to exorcise them, to appease them, to bribe them, and to rob them of part of their power by thus influencing them." Rebellion against institutionalized religion does exist, however; most movements against it have been initiated by powerful men like the Borgias, who virtually made Luther, rather than by Satanists, or heretics like Frank.

The ontological phase of personality development culminates in the formation of a separate self and of an ego boundary between the ego and his surroundings. A faulty or malformed ego boundary may predispose a person to some forms of ego disorganization; as we have already noted, there are some justifications for regarding defects in personality structure as deviance from social norms, and viewing mental aberrations, not as disease entities, but as a breakdown in interaction with relevant others (7). As for the complex processes that may lead to a malformed ego boundary, it is sufficient to say for the purposes of this book that ego pathology may be linked to gross inconsistencies in parental attitudes and behavior toward the child. If their relationship with the child is marked at the outset by utter confusion, he will not have any consistent pattern of reactions on which to base his ego boundary. If the directives he gets from his relationship with his parents are amorphous and ambiguous, his ego boundary will at best be fragmentary, and at worst almost nonexistent.

The predisposition to deviance of such a person may, at the inner-directed extreme, take the form of autistic catatonia. He feels under constant pressure; he longs to dissolve his weak ego boundary, because he cannot take it any more, he cannot hold out any longer. When the breakdown does come, he very often feels relief, as if the dissolution of his personality means he reverts to a "natural" state, against which his ego boundary was an artificial barrier.

A predisposition to catatonic morbidity gives a special meaning to manifestations of losing control over one's self. These patients accept the inevitable annihilation of the self as result of battle; they are weary of the necessity of pretending to be sane, weary of propriety—whatever that means to their family—weary of being what they are not. They embrace the freedom to be mad at last, and to cast off the artificial and their fragmentary ego boundary. They are like tired and starving mountain climbers who welcome the fatal embrace of the engulfing snows that eventually will freeze them to death. This desire for annihilation of the self has been interpreted as proof of the death instinct; from the viewpoint of social psychology, these patients may be described as people who have done their best, but whose weak or nonexistent ego boundaries have finally crumbled.

The predisposition to paranoia which is the outwardly-directed reaction of such a person is linked to interactive relationships with relevant others that produce a negative ego boundary. Basically, this means that a "me" is formed that is surrounded by evil and badness. Negative transmissions and labelling by the relevant others in the family and outside it are internalized by the child, who forms an initial "bad me" self-concept. The child eventually projects his aggression toward everybody and everything in his environment. This projection of aggressiveness may assume delusional dimensions. A negative and a threatening world drives the "me" into a series of defensive moves which seem to allow him to cope with all the menacing forces that threaten to destroy him. The greater the delusions and the fiercer the hallucinatory persecution, the stronger the corresponding delusions of grandeur. Each new proof of the world's persecution is accompanied by an "I told you so" kind of self-satisfaction, and followed by a flow of uncontrolled rage. This violent hyperactivity is more often than not a developmental stage; usually the escalating aggression reaches such a height of impotent rage and anger that it leads to a complete breakdown and exhaustion.

Moral awakening comes when ego identity synchronizes the individual's reciprocal expectations with his relevant others. Here, flaws in socialization may express themselves in conflict situations, as, for example, when ideals of goodness are contradicted by the actual unlawful and immoral behavior of the parents. Also, even overt moral behavior may be contradicted by subliminal parental aggression, which may be eagerly absorbed by the children. This type of situation often is translated by the child into direct and immediate expression; he may reject the abstract and symbolic indoctrinations, and absorb or imitate the parental mandates transmitted to him by their actual behavior or gestures. Stigmatizing processes, and the absorption by the child of negative tags with which he fashions a negative social image—that is, his ego identity—are almost inevitable in these circumstances.

Another type of conflict situation arises when the child is socialized through grossly inconsistent norms, so that the adolescent has only a hazy notion about what is expected of him. This type of conflict situation is often linked to a fragmentary ego identity or one that is very diffuse. The manifestations of deviance that may result include most of the official crimes in a given society. When an adolescent with a hazy ego identity is the inner-directed type, he may become an individualized criminal, corresponding to the noncareer criminal of Dunhum and Lindesmith's typology (8). This type of offender is not a member of a gang or a deviant sub-culture; his offenses are a manifestation of his personal pathologies. He commits his deviant acts alone without the help or company of other criminals. When the adolescent is outer-directed, he becomes a social criminal (9). He becomes a member of the criminal group, fully absorbing its norms and values and rejecting the norms of legitimate society. He regards crime as a way of life, as a profession, and a vocation.

The Social Factors

The social factors that must be considered in discussing deviance are the family unit, ecological and economic factors, culture conflicts, social disorganization, and anomie.

In the case of the criminal family, the learning of deviance begins at home, where the primary socialization contains criminal and deviant patterns. The kind and degree of criminal socialization varies, from the criminal tribes or castes in India where the primary criminal socialization is normative (10), to families in which one or more members have a deviant history or are actively engaged in crime. Research findings have indicated that the chances of another member of the family becoming delinquent are overwhelmingly higher in these families than in families which do not have any criminal or deviant member.

Homes broken by divorce, separation, death, and

prolonged incapacitation have also been found to be significantly linked with juvenile delinquency and deviance (11). Inadequate families marked by unhappy, conflict-ridden homes, tension, irritation, quarrels, and friction between parents, resulting in inconsistent treatment, ambivalence, and violently alternating attitudes toward the children, were also found to be strongly linked with delinquency and deviance (12).

Causal links have been established between crime and deviance and conflict ridden homes (13); the feminization of modern socialization agencies (14,15); post-adolescent maladjustment (16,17); and conspicuous consumption (18,19,20,21). Lack of cohesion of the family unit and the slackening of parental control (22) have been found to be especially relevant to the delinquency of the first-generation children of immigrant parents.

Ecological factors. The study of the ecology of crime, delinquency, and deviance has been revived by Shaw and MacKay, the Chicago school (23), by Morris in England (24), and by Christiansen in Denmark (25). An Israeli study showed that the rates of juvenile delinquency increase with rising urbanization as measured by density of population and the volume of commerce and industry (26).

In general, these studies have found that the rate of serious crimes tends to increase with the size of the community as measured by the number of its inhabitants. Conversely, the number of crimes decreases with distance from the large cities. The crime rates are highest in the low-rent and low-status areas near the city, and in the industrial and commercial centers. (27) The business and social associations of the various criminal groups tend to converge on these high crime and deviance areas, with the result that the ecology of deviance is closely related to certain specific urban areas.

Economic factors. Research into the possible link between poverty and crime has always been a part of scientific criminology. These efforts may be divided into two opposing schools. At one extreme there is the Marxist point of view, as voiced in Bouger's classic work (28), according to which all crimes, murder and rape included, can be linked to poverty. At the other extreme is Ferri's point of view that affluence and economic prosperity are positively related to crime (29). The studies range in sophistication from crude measurements of the relationship between economic conditions and crimes—Von Mayrs' one-pfenning-per-bushel increase in the price of rye in Bavaria (30), to Sellins' indices for economic growth and decline as related to various types of law infringements (31).

Economic need may be measured objectively, but greed is a subjective state; and crime and deviance are more often related to greed than to need. An Indian who is starving to death might not regard himself as needy enough to kill one of the sacred cows and fry himself a steak. On the other hand, a man who cannot afford to buy a mink coat for his mistress may define his situation as needy enough to embezzle the necessary funds from his employer. In addition, as Reckless has pointed out the curve of economic conditions and crime may well be bimodal, with lower-class and upper-income levels as the modes, and the middleclass at the lowest point.

On the other hand, there is some evidence to show that it is a mistake to relate either poverty or affluence to crime and delinquency, and that instead the important factor may be the effects of conflict situations on the socializing process, especially on norms that form an initial barrier against criminal and deviant solutions. These norms relate to the sanctity of private property and abstention from violence as a means of solving disputes. These norms, when transmitted effectively by the parents, were the significant factors differentiating nondelinquent boys from delinquent gang members who were exposed to the same economic conditions.

The idea that family controls are more important as barriers against delinquency and crime than economic conditions by themselves, may partly explain the higher rate of delinquency among some ethnic groups whose family structure is for various historical reasons generally different from the modal type of family. It may also clarify one crucial criminological question—why, even in the worst slums plagued by poverty, bad living conditions, criminal gangs, prostitutes, and dope peddlers, do only some boys become delinquent, whereas the far greater number remain law-abiding?

Culture Conflicts. Many criminologists regard economic conditions in the United States and Europe at the base of the class, ethnic, and other social stratification factors of crime and delinquency. This point of view has been negated by studies made in developing countries and in societies undergoing rapid social change—for instance, Israel. In these countries the cultural lag or cultural gap between the various ethnic groups seemed to be more important than economic factors.

If we take, for instance, as one measure, the length of stay in the country, the cultural gap between the first-generation newcomers and the absorbing community will be wide and the areas of normative friction will consequently be low. With the second generation the cultural rapprochement will produce far greater opportunities for friction and conflict, which may account for the fact that the highest rates of delinquency occurred among the second-generation youngsters of immigrant parentage. With the third generation, when integration within the absorbing community has more or less been accomplished, the ethnic groups of low economic status are highly oriented toward achievement and overconformity with the receiving community. This development has been observed in the United States, for example, where the third generation of immigrant stock is apt to display zealous attachment to the norms of the American way of life, and to overconform to the normative system as a whole.

The main problems of culture conflicts with respect to crime, deviance, and immigration therefore arise with the second generation. The native-born of immigrant parentage, or those who came very young, are the most apt to suffer from the effects of their parents' immigration, since the conduct norms of their parents usually diverge from the prevailing norms in the receiving country. The process of integration may also injure and sometimes shatter the social and economic status of the head of the family. This and other effects of the process of integration may weaken the cohesion of the family unit, and thus hamper family control over the young.

Social Disorganization and Anomie. Anomie is a predisposition to deviance because most of the norms of the criminal law are an integral part of the normative system of societies. Anomic trends in societies are indeed universal, although different in scale and degree. A society may suffer from simple anomie, characterized by conflict among the various belief systems (ideologies); or it may be plagued by acute anomie, involving a severe deterioration of religious, political and other ideological systems which ultimately produce the disintegration of its structure (32).

The Dynamic Processes of Association

Triggering processes that initiate the individual's association with deviant patterns of behavior serve as a link between the personal and social factors predisposing to deviance. These dynamic processes also include the pressures toward deeper deviance that culminate in the formation of the deviant subculture.

According to Daniel Glaser (33), before a person

actually associates with the criminal or deviant group, he may identify with criminal images and play deviant roles—that is, before he actually behaves as a criminal, he adopts criminal values and roles and sees himself as a criminal or deviant. The delinquent image of being smart (34) "involves the capacity to outsmart, outfox, outwit, dupe, 'take', 'con' another or others, and the concomitant capacity to avoid being outwitted, 'taken', or duped oneself." The status aspired to and the image identified with is often that of a big shot driving a big car, wearing flashy suits, with a lot of money, and surrounded by beautiful women. After he identifies with criminal images, the potential deviant must have access to illegitimate or deviant structures, some opportunity for criminal association that gives him avenues to illegitimate and deviant occupations (35).

The overt initiation into the life of crime or deviance thus involves association with deviant groups and their patterns of behavior. Although learning by associating with deviant patterns of behavior is presumably confined to property offenders, learning by association may also explain compulsive crimes, like kleptomania (36). Similar processes of learning have been observed in prostitution (37), homosexuality, and drug addiction (38).

Many of the situational aspects of deviance are part of the dynamic processes of deviance. We may take as an example the murder described by Wolfgang (39): "A drunken husband, beating his wife in their kitchen, gave her a butcher's knife and dared her to use it on him. She claimed that if he struck her once more, she would use the knife. He slapped her face and she stabbed him—to death." This excerpt describes only the last phase of a violent exchange of words and actions between husband and wife which culminated in death.

Most attempts to explain murder try to identify specific factors which might single out the slayer from other human beings. The biologists look for physiological irregularities, abnormal blood chemistry, or perhaps XYY chromosomes. Psychoanalysts look for unresolved complexes in the development of the personality. Sociologists pursue correlations between murder and bad homes, bad schools, and bad neighborhoods. All such explanations are genetic or historical. However, a situational explanation of murder considers it to be the culmination of an escalation of tension and violence. This approach has been described by Sutherland (40):

> Scientific explanations of criminal behavior may be stated either in terms of the processes which are operating at the moment of the occurrence of the crime or in terms of the processes operating in the earlier history of the criminal. In the first case, the explanation may be called "mechanistic," "situational" or "dynamic," in the second "historical" or "genetic" . . . . Criminological explanations of the mechanistic type have thus been notably unsuccessful, perhaps largely because they have been formulated in connection with the attempt to isolate personal and social pathologies among criminals. Work from this point of view has, at best, resulted in the conclusion that the immediate determinants of criminal behavior lie in the person-situation complex.

The situational approach thus attempts to explain the deviant act in terms of the criminal-victim relationship. In some types of violence, for instance, personality and demographic factors are relevant predisposing factors. Apart from the physiological factors predisposing to low boiling points, some measureable personality traits may also contribute to violence-proneness. On the other hand, someone with a very firm inner-directedness who would consider any infringement upon his internalized standards as very hard to take, would very rarely interpret what someone else might say as a provocation because such statements would be extraneous to his internal controls.

Even if a predisposition to violence could be expressed as probability profiles that would point out the low or high chances of an individual displaying a given set of characteristics related to committing a violent act, the actual sequence of events precipitating the violence will often undoubtedly be caused by the interaction between criminal and victim. Such a pattern of communication might involve a compromising situation—for example, a faithless wife and her lover discovered by the husband, or perhaps insulting words obviously meant to offend. They have the effect of switching an individual's action to a different cognitive level, of making him see red. Situational factors tend to trigger violence when they are defined as humiliating. The conventional form of an offensive gesture may have an even stronger escalatory effect. Such an exchange of words and gestures may not trigger off immediate arousal to another cognitive level, but, depending on the reaction, may gradually lead to the point of no return where violence flares.

Theories on deviant sub-culture formation may be divided into three groups. First are the theories centered on class, that stress the clashes of class structures, and the discrepancies between the normative system of the upper and middle classes, and the performance level of lowerclass youth. Representative of this group are the works of Albert Cohen (41) and of Whyte (42), Miller (43), and Cloward and Ohlin (44). Second are the theories that have linked delinquent and deviant processes to flaws in primary socialization, advanced by Thrasher (45), Bloch and Neiderhoffer (46), and Erikson (47). A third group of theorists see the delinquent gang as an expression of normative discord among individuals and groups in society, among whom are Merton (48), Tannenbaum (49), Zorbaugh (50), Kvaraceus (51), and Matza (52).

The class-centered studies were pioneered by Albert Cohen. He regards the delinquent subculture as a result of the discrepancy between middleclass norms and the achievement level of lowerclass boys. His assumption is quite feasible—that society must have some place to put the lowerclass rejects and failures, the laggards of the rat race whose rules are made by middle and upperclass elites.

Whyte's study of the gangs in the Italian slum in Cornerville has been incorporated by Cloward and Ohlin; their theory is that a lowerclass or slum youth may have limited access to legitimate opportunities, this makes him aware that illegitimate opportunities are available, so that he tries to find access to them.

Cloward and Ohlin distinguish three different sub-cultures whose sociological function and structure vary. The first is the criminal sub-culture, mainly property offenses. Here the sub-culture inmates have been rejected from structures of legitimate opportunity, while the road leading from a relatively organized slum to the illegitimate opportunity structures is wide open. The delinquent sub-culture is linked with adult organized crime through a liaison man, usually the fence. The young delinquent sub-culture thus serves as a recruiting depot for the adult underworld.

The second delinquent sub-culture is one of conflict and violence. Violent gangs are detached both from the legitimate and illegitimate structures. Usually they are not eligible for either because of language, ethnic origin, or some other socioeconomic barrier. They form a delusional world of kings, dragons, and magicians, and carve out territories for themselves where fights can be held and status gained without resort to the inaccessible adult world.

The third delinquent sub-culture is retreatist. These are youths who have been rejected by and in turn have rejected legitimate achievement. They either have inner normative barriers against joining the illegitimate structure, or have also been rejected by the latter so that they are double failures. Their solution is a collective fringe existence, where they are mainly interested in kicks, and a temporary and increasingly expensive euphoria.

Miller's theory on the formation of the delinquent subculture is based on the seemingly far-fetched contention that part of the normative system of the lower classes in itself is geared toward law violation. These "criminal norms" become the nucleus for a normative system for the delinquent subculture. "Engaging in certain cultural practices which comprise essential elements of the total life pattern of lowerclass culture *automatically* violate certain legal norms" (53). Where Cohen sees the delinquent subculture as the outcome of a clash between the lowerclass boys' performance level and middleclass norms, Miller regards part of the lowerclass normative system in *itself* as delinquent.

Thrasher's theory of inadequate socialization views the gang as a substitute for the failing socializing agencies. Where and when the family, school, church, and other agencies fail to hold, attract, and regulate the necessities and leisure time, be it out of neglect, repression, or inadequacy, the youth unite spontaneously to form an alternative existence by themselves and for themselves—that is, the gang.

Bloch and Niederhoffer, on the other hand, trace the delinquency of both lower and middleclass youths to a faulty adolescence. Their hypothesis is based partly on Erikson's theory of personality, according to which the end product of a socialized and "adjusted" adult is ego identity, that is, "a persistent sameness within oneself and a persistent sharing of some kind of essential character with others." The period of adolescence is characterized by ego diffusion, which manifests itself by a diffused sense of time, vanity, and an inability to develop deep intimacy with other human beings, continuous experimentation in various roles, both on a real basis and in day dreams, and uncompromising and belligerent loyalty to ideas.

An adolescent in this state of ego diffusion may be ripe for gang membership because it often helps him to act, and reinforces his sense of identity. His assignments in the gang overcome his feelings of vacillation and paralysis; and as a gang member, he can safely assert his masculinity and his defiance of authority.

Merton's classic exposition of the various disjunctures between goals and institutionalized norms and means to achieve them has been used as the basis of various theories on the formation of deviant subcultures.

Merton's typology, in a modified version, may be used to describe the outward manifestations of some criminal and deviant groups. The criminal, crime-for-gain group, for instance, is characterized by the acquisition for property or other material objects—that is, an accepted cultural goal reached by illicit means. The retreatist subculture is characterized by the rejection of goals, norms, and means; instead it pursues hedonistic pleasures, drugs and alcohol. The violent groups are chaotic rebels, aggressive, restless youths whose goals are not very clear. These are, to be sure, only external descriptions of the activities of each of these groups. Of deeper relevance to the formation of criminal and deviant groups is Merton's statement (54) that: "What the individual experiences as estrangement from a group of which he is a member tends to be experienced by his associates as repudiation of the group, and this ordinarily evokes a hostile response." This hostile response eventually helps to unite the rejects into their own subculture.

Zorbaugh describes a similar process in his study, reporting that when the boy's family or neighborhood are defined for him as "dago," "wop," or "foreign," that by "these same *definitive epithets, he is excluded from status and intimate participation* in American life. Out of this situation arises the gang. By conforming to delinquent patterns he achieves status in the gang, and every boy in Little Hell is a member of a gang."

Among the most recent theoretical expositions of normative discord are the works of Kvaraceus and Matza. Kvaraceus claims that the modern social structure makes youth a surplus, a superfluous commodity (55):

> Automation with its elimination of routine chores that once depended upon youthful hands, labor laws written in the spirit of safeguarding children and youth, and labor unions organized to protect the adult worker, have all combined to diminish the needs for strong young hands. Even the compulsory classroom, now extending through the teen-age years, has tended to shunt the young learners from the main stream of social, civic and economic life activity of family and community, thereby retarding the process whereby youth join the adult world. In a sense, the young now experience an organized isolation from the regular community.

Youth becomes, therefore, the modern involuntary leisure class, with an excess of leisure. Forced leisure becomes the social and structural background of modern delinquent and deviant groups. This theoretical premise was advanced long ago in the *Talmud:* "Loafing is the mother of all vice."

General social conditions, however, cannot be confused with the actual dynamics of delinquent and deviant group formation. Kvaraceus goes on to point out that one of the possible outcomes of the structural superfluity of modern youth is that they are excluded by the adult world from significant roles and tasks; these are now scarce becoming scarcer with the spread of technology and specialization. The youths feel unneeded and unnecessary, and worst of all, they are infantilized and ignored. One of the things they can do to make themselves feel better is to form their own membership and reference groups, the gangs.

Sherif (56) supports Kvaraceus's conclusions by describing the youth's sense of deprivation, insecurity, and the feeling of being tossed around by the adults; these emotions disappear entirely once a youngster joins the gang, and anchors himself in a sympathetic peer group of kindred souls. Matza seems to assume, however, that the delinquent simply drifts through a permissive environment, in a normative vacuum. This is not true. No one is left alone to drift; we are all jostled, coerced, and pushed around by society. We are required to commit ourselves: either you are with the legitimate structure, or not, in which case you are by definition against it. Matza (57) does point out that the delinquent "is transformed in the situation of company to a committed delinquent by dint of the cues he has received from others." This is actually an internalization of an image thrust upon the delinquent by adults, and sometimes by his square peers.

Les plus déspérés sont les
chants les plus beaux.

ALFRED DE MUSSET

CHAPTER **VI**

THE

USES

OF

DEVIANCE

As I pointed out in Chapter I, the Social Darwinists, the Structuralists, and prominent sociologists like Parsons, Merton, and Lundberg regard conflict, change and deviance as a dysfunction—a kind of disease in the structure of society or in one of its systems. Diametrically opposed to this value judgment of these followers of Durkheim are the followers of another old-world sage, George Simmel— Park, Burgess, and especially Coser. They believe in the functionality of conflicts: that is, that conflicts are good for you, and that change means progress for society.

The Dialectics of Social Conflict

Dialectics should not be thought of as a pendulum that swings between a static Hell and a static Heaven;

rather it is more like a surge from one temporary balance to another, a movement generated by the pressures of conflicting forces. Marx admitted that conflicts within a class may be dissipated by the exigencies of interclass struggles. That is, friendship may be defined in terms of common enemies. Coser (1), in his analysis of the functionality of social conflicts, offers a number of examples of this theme of cohesion and renewal of the group through conflict. He describes how outside dangers enhance the morale and unity of the group; how in-group conflicts may dissolve "dysfunctional" norms, and establish more vital ones; and how power struggles may focus or redefine the balance of power. However, the crucial question still remains: when is a disrupting conflict (which is by definition a form of deviance) "functional," "dialectic," and "good" to the structure; and when does it lead to destruction, decay, and anomie?

This question is relevant only for conflict theorists, because Durkheim and his disciples regard every disruption as anomic. Its rule of thumb answer is that when conflicts disrupt the structure in such a way that realization of the basic goals and functions of the structure becomes impossible or unfeasible, the conflictual change is anomic. On the other hand, when the conflictual change merely reshuffles the norms and means without jeopardizing the goals, it may be deemed a dialectical adjustment. Coser also adds that the chances of a conflict being functional and dialectic are better when the structure is flexible. If the structure is rigid, the probabilities are higher that a conflictual change will lead to an anomic rupture.

The conflict theorists join Marx, Marcuse, and Fanon in advocating the disruption of present states, because anything new would be better, more progressive, and more advanced. The destruction of normative walls, regarded as disaster by the adjustment-based theorists, is from the viewpoint of conflict dialecticians only a necessary step toward desirable change; they consider this a step forward, toward a given goal and not away from it.

The functionality of conflicts is one of the oldest modes of justifying strife. "Homer was wrong when he prayed that strife might perish from among gods and men. He did not see that he was praying for the destruction of the universe, for if his prayer was heard all things would pass away . . . . Man does not know how what is at variance agrees with itself. It is an attunement of opposite tensions, like that of the bow and the lyre" (2). This idea of conciliation among disjunctures was part of the thought of Kant, Hegel, Marx, and Freud. Freud even defined psychoanalysis as a "dynamic conception which reduces mental life to the interplay of reciprocally urging and checking forces" (3). It is the avenue of least resistance for the contradictory forces of history as well as the petty inconsistencies of everyday life. Most of the phenomena involving inconsistent normative pressures—from emotional ambivalence to class conflict—have been explained by the functionality of conflict.

In its application to deviance, the basic notion that two contradictory or inconsistent states are resolved into a congruous third state implies that every new normative disjuncture is perceived as a novel task, an incentive for activity and creativity. Creativity thus becomes a process of catharsis, and accomplishment occurs through the need to overcome a block. Normative disjunctures may, no doubt, be perceived by individuals as obstacles to be overcome by creative efforts. As Freud said (4), the libido soars to heights of expression only by the process of forcing itself through barriers, and the stronger the barrier, the richer the ensuing creativity. "It requires an obstacle to drive the libido up to a high point, and where the natural obstacles to satisfaction are not sufficient, men have at all times interposed conventional ones to be able to enjoy love." Moreover, Freud imputes the creation of culture to the human sense of guilt, including the genesis of law and order, and also religion and art.

The widest application, however, of the functionality of deviance is in ethics and social interaction.

Plotinus (5) asserted as a principle considered ancient even in his time, that otherness and sameness help to define and emphasize each other. The socially conforming are defined by contrast with the socially deviant, the law-abiding by the criminal, and the socially in through the exclusion of the nondeserving outs. "People like us" need the criminal in order to assert through him their image of righteousness. In psychoanalytic terminology the quest for primitive justice—that is, the al-

compare

location of evil to the criminal, to whom it belongs—reinforces the superego of the righteous. The darker he is, the brighter they shine. Criminals, deviants, and pariahs serve also to drain off legitimate citizens' overflow of aggression—hence the festive curiosity in the courtroom, and the interest in crime reports in the newspapers.

As a direct corollary of this reasoning, innovators are perceived as harbingers of desired and "progressive" social change. But innovators, by definition, are deviants. They have special qualities, unusual insights, and subtlety of perception, all qualities that almost guarantee they will be labeled deviant. Consequently, innovator-deviants are responsible for much of the progress of society and culture, in the Spencerian sense. The sad part of this story is that the group usually repays the innovators with ostracism, sometimes even death—only to raise monuments to their memory afterwards. It is an open question whether the innovator is first labeled deviant and then becomes one; or whether due to his social marginality he is pressed toward innovation because the conventional avenues of opportunity are blocked to him (6).

The criminal serves the legitimate society in many ways. First, he allows the law-abiding bourgeois to release some of his aggression. This release of aggression used to be served by public hangings and floggings; nowadays we have the enormous publicity given to crimes and punishments by the press, radio, and television. There is a striking similarity between the fights of

Roman gladiators, bullfights, prizefights, and criminal trials. The battle between the defense and prosecution in the tense and exciting atmosphere of the courtroom, especially in sensational cases, turns the criminal process into a festivity fueled by repressed aggression, perverse curiosity, and oftentimes latent or overt sadism. Hatred and righteousness felt toward the criminal by law-abiding citizens may help legitimate society to strengthen its norms through denunciation of their violators. As Lord Denning says (7):

> The punishment inflicted for grave crimes should adequately reflect the revulsion felt by the great majority of citizens for them. The ultimate justification of any punishment is the emphatic denunciation by the community of a crime. But actually the righteous indignation towards the criminal is also the releasing, the "living out" of the aggressive impulse of legislators, judicial officers, prosecuting attorneys, police, juries and the public.

Punishing the criminal also helps to ease the guilt felt by respectable citizens. Man's life is riddled with endless normative proscriptions, moral, social and legal. The constant inner struggle, and especially the desire to act against these morals and laws create conflicts that are eased by righteously punishing criminals. The retributive penalty inflicted on the criminal who has committed acts we secretly wish to do symbolically expiates our own guilt for dreaming of the same behavior.

The criminal and his punishment also help the

respectable and law-abiding citizen to remain respectable and law-abiding; if the criminal is not punished properly, the squares will think, "Why should I fight my natural tendencies to commit an immoral or criminal act when those who ignore the law only steal things that I want myself, get off lightly. There ought to be heavy penalties!" This explains why the first stones are very rarely cast by those who are without sin. The stronger a man's antisocial tendencies, the fiercer may be his righteous demand that offenders should be punished. The most ardent moralizers may strongly sympathize on an unconscious level with the immoral deeds. In psychoanalytic terms, the more a person's hatred *and effective negativism* toward criminals, the weaker is his superego apt to be in his battle with his own aggressions, asociality, and immorality. "The underworld and its official prosecutors show not infrequently a subterranean affinity" (8). The criminal's detection, apprehension, and punishment help, therefore, legitimate society to check its aggressions, curb latent criminal tendencies, and ease guilt feelings.

Even detective stories illustrate this point. Aggressive and antisocial tendencies are aroused when we consciously or subconsciously identify with the criminal in these books. The identification causes guilt feelings; to overcome these and to prove once again that crime does not pay, Sherlock Holmes, Perry Mason, and Maigret are always successful, the law is victorious, the criminal is first found, then hanged or imprisoned, and everyone lives happily ever after. Or take, as another example, sexual offenders. Modern culture is replete with sex stimuli—literature, art, movies, posters, advertisements are full of them. At the same time, cultural repression of sexual attitudes is equally strong. The ensuing conflict is somewhat eased by vehement denunciations of sex fiends and sexual maniacs. "No one," says Weihofen (9), "is more bitter in condemning the 'loose' woman than the 'good' women, who have on occasion guiltily enjoyed some purple dreams themselves."

Last but not least, the denuciation of an outgroup (the criminals) always help the cohesion of the ingroup. There is no better way to arouse solidarity in a citizen's action committee than a vivid description of a threatening crime wave. The most potent part of a norm is the sanction for not complying with it. Using this sanction on violators strengthens the force of the norm, and demonstrates to everyone that the law is not an empty word, but a whip with a stinging lash.

Genet, with his customary exaggeration and dramatic flourish, sees other social uses for the criminal. According to him, the judge needs the criminal much more than the criminal needs the judge. The Judge in *The Balcony,* for instance, realizes that his identity depends on his being able to declare thieves to be thieves and treat them accordingly. "My being a Judge," he tells the prostitute-thief, "is an emanation of your being a thief. . . If I no longer had to divide the Good from the Evil, what use would I be?" Genet believes that a thief gives an ethical anchor to the world. He offers a wonderful service to the legitimate world, since he provides the criterion (a false one, of course) for dividing black from white. "A judge, I'm going to be judge of your acts! On me depends the weighing, the balance. The world is an apple; I cut it in two! The good, the bad. And you agree, thank you, you agree to be the bad." Without criminals, Genet says, there are no judges, no punishment, and no condemnation; yet to condemn is the essence of judges and justice. It is as if the criminals owe the judges their crime, so that they can mete out a just desert, and so perform their function.

Social deviants seem to be as useful to the normative structure of the group, as well as to the well-being of its conforming members, as formal criminals are. In many societies the existence of some safety-valve mechanisms, like prostitution, help preserve the family unit (10). The "career fool" may help the group by serving to release stifling tensions (11). The deviant may be the social glue which unites a whole group, because they all share concern about his problems (12). Also, the deviant may focus his activities on some vulnerability of the group's structure or normative system which would otherwise have remained undetected.

The deviant also serves the group through projection and displacement. Projection is the directing outward of ego's own subjective states; in deviance, these are aggression and negation. Displacement occurs when ego imputes his own inner states to the wrong objects or sources—in this context, the misdirection of the stigmatizer's own frustration, aggression, and resentment to those he labels as deviant. Both projection and displacement are defense mechanisms vital to the preservation of equilibrium and sanity. Attributing frustration and failure to one's own self, no matter how valid the attribution, can be damaging and sometimes disastrous. People cannot bear to face the truth on a cognitive level, so they displace their intolerable attributes on to some convenient and symbolically relevant others. Projection and displacement transference are basically defense mechanisms of individuals in interaction; often the recipients of these mechanisms are the deviants.

Scapegoating of deviants can be traced to the ancient rites of the displacement of evil on to inanimate objects, other people, and gods. Frazer (13) gives many examples of the displacement of evil on to a human scapegoat, who thereby carries the evil away from the individual or group. The god who dies as scapegoat is a figure of many ancient and primitive societies; the legend reaches its peak with Christ. Stoning is another way evil and guilt are displaced on to a human scapegoat. Everyone in the stoning group symbolically transfers the evil by throwing a stone from himself to the presumed source of the evil, the man being stoned (14).

John Steinbeck (15) offers another example of displacement in a conversation with a farmer:

"You think then we might be using the Russians as an outlet for something else, for other things?"

"I didn't think that at all sir, but I bet I'm going to. Why, I remember when people took everything out on Mr. Roosevelt. Andy Larsen got red in the face about Roosevelt one time when his hens got the croup. Yes sir," he said with growing enthusiasm, "those Russians got quite a load to carry. Man, had a fight with his wife, he belts the Russians. Maybe everybody needs Russians. I'll bet even in Russia they need Russians, maybe they call it Americans."

The value of scapegoating a whole group is clear enough. An enemy of the people can be an individual, or an individual may transfer and generalize his hatred to a whole group. What is important is that displacement tends to channel the hatred and resentment bred by frustration and failure toward a deviant individual or a deviant group.

Finally, the deviant, the heretic, and the sinner have been exhaustively utilized by religious institutions. According to the *Kabbalah,* free-floating evil and sin prevents salvation. The Messiah absorbs the sins of the community, and becomes polluted thereby. The Shabbateans took this a step further and proclaimed that the Messiah "had to behave in an adverse and deviant manner in order to be scolded by the Wise" (16). The Savior has to be degraded on purpose in order to be outwardly fit for the role of the scapegoat, the absorber of filth and sin. The polluted Messiah has to be scolded and slandered so that "Israel may sing and rejoice." This led to the logical sequence that sin, deviance, and sacrilege, if performed in the proper context, are holy and sacred.

The "usefulness" of crime and deviance, and their punishment is thus the same for religious as it is for secular squares. The absorption of sin by the savior is an archetypal image equivalent to the role of the scapegoat and the stigmatized. The stigmatizer projects his pent-up aggression; the family scapegoat serves as a receptacle for the guilt and frustration of the family members. By transferring to the scapegoat his own inner craving for deviance and promiscuity, the stigmatizer is cleansed of his evil desire. Once again, the deviant's relationship to the group is to offer salvation through pollution.

References to Chapter I

1. E. Goffman, *Stigma*. Englewood Cliffs, N. J.: Prentice Hall, 1963.

2. A. V. Gouldner, "Anti-Minotaur: The Myth of Value-Free Sociology," *Social Problems*, 9 (1962), 199.

3. E. Durkheim, *The Division of Labour in Society*, Glencoe, Ill.: Free Press, 1947, 163.

4. G. Nettler, "Antisocial Sentiment and Criminality," *Am. Soc. Rev.* (1959), 202-08.

5. L. A. Coser, *The Functions of Social Conflict*, Glencoe, Ill.: Free Press, 1956.

6. J. P. Sartre, *Being and Nothingness*, London: Methuen, 1957, 23.

7. H. Silving, "Suicide and Law," in H. S. Shneidman and N. L. Farberow (eds.), *Clues to Suicide*, New York: McGraw-Hill, 1957, 81.

8. J. G. Frazer, *Folklore in the Old Testament*, London: MacMillan, 1919, Chapter III.

9. H. von Hentig, *Punishment,* London 1935, 117 ff.; also, G. Ives, *A History of Penal Methods,* London, 1914, 78 ff.

10. J. G. Peristiany, in E. E. Pritchard, *The Institutions of Primitive Society,* Oxford: Basil Blackwell, 1954.

11. W. G. Summer, *Folkways,* Boston: Ginn & Co., 1934, 219.

12. The ideological bases of this school of thought were laid down in the 18th-Century by de Beccaria in Italy and Feuerbach in Germany.

13. J. Lange, *Crime as Destiny,* New York: Boni, 1930.

14. S. Kretschmer, *Physique and Character,* New York: The Humanities Press, 1949.

15. A. Drahms, *The Criminal, His Person and Environment,* New York: Macmillan, 1900.

16. G. J. Mohr and R. H. Gundlach, "A Further Study of the Relations Between Physique and Performance in Criminals," *J. Ab. & Soc. Psych.,* 24 (1929-30).

17. E. A. Hooton, *The American Criminal, An Anthropological Study.* Cambridge, Mass.: 1939.

18. C. Goring, *The English Convict, A Statistical Study,* London: HMSO, 1913.

19. H. Mannheim, *Comparative Criminology,* London: Routledge, Kegan Paul, 1965, Chapter II.

20. M. F. Ashley Montagu, "The Biologist Looks at Crime," *Annals of the Academy of Political and Social Science,* 1941, 46-57.

21. W. N. East, *Society and the Criminal,* London: HMSO, 1940.

22. K. Friedlander, *The Psychoanalytical Approach to Juvenile Delinquency,* London: Routledge, Kegan Paul, 1947.

23. M. Woodward, *Low Intelligence & Crime,* London: ISTD, 1955.

24. W. and J. McCord, *Psychopathy and Delinquency,* New York, 1956.

25. S. and E. Glueck (eds.), *Unravelling Juvenile Delinquency,* New York: The Commonwealth Fund, 1950.

26. E. H. Sutherland and D. R. Cressey, *Principles of Criminology.* Philadelphia: Lippincott, 1970.

27. A. R. Lindesmith, *Opiate Addiction.* Bloomington, Ind.: Principle Press, 1947.

28. H. D. G. Lewis, *A Short History of Psychiatric Achievement.* New York: Norton, 1941.

29. G. Zilboorg and G. W. Henry, *A History of Medical Psychology.* New York: Norton, 1941.

30. H. S. Sullivan, *Clinical Studies in Psychiatry.* New York: Norton, 1956.

31. P. Mullahy, "Harry Stack Sullivan's Theory of Schizophrenia," *International Journal of Psychiatry,* 4 (1967), 492.

32. S. Shoham, *The Mark of Cain,* New York: Oceana Publishing, 1969.

33. A. Crowcroft, *The Psychotic.* London: Penguin Books, 1967.

34. P. Halmos, *Towards a Measure of Man.* London: Routledge, Kegan Paul, 1957.

35. M. D. Bogdonoff, R. F. Klein, E. H. Estes, M. M. Shaw, and K. W. Back, "The Modifying Effect of Conforming Behaviour Upon Lipid Responses Accompanying CNC Arousal," *Clin. Res.,* 9 (1961), 135.

36. R. Brown, *Social Psychology,* Glencoe, Ill.: The Free Press, 1966, 678-79.

37. Krech, Crutchfield and Ballachey, *Individuals in Society.* New York: McGraw-Hill, 1962, 525-26.

38. J. Bensman, I. Gerber. "Crime and Punishment in the Factory," *Am. Soc. Rev.,* 28 (1963), 588-98.

39. A. Cohen, *Deviance and Control.* Englewood Cliffs, N. J.: Prentice-Hall, 1966, 25.

References to Chapter II

1. W. J. Thibaut and H. H. Kelley, *The Social Psychology of Groups,* New York: Wiley, 1959, 239.

2. L. Kohlberg, *Stage and Sequence: The Developmental Approach to Moralization,* New York: Holt, Rinehart & Winston, 1969.

3. R. Rommetveit, *Social Norms and Roles,* Minneapolis, Minn.: Univ. of Minnesota Press, 1954, 45.

4. T. Sellin, *Culture-Conflict and Crime,* New York: Social Science Research Council, 1938, 34, ff.

5. Thibaut, and Kelley, 239.

6. L. C. Wynne, I. M. Ryckoff, J. Day, and S. I. Hirsch, "Pseudo Mutuality in the Family Relations of Schizophrenia," in N. W. Bell, and E. P. Vogel (eds.) *A Modern Introduction to the Family.* Glencoe, Ill.: Free Press, 1968, 573.

7. S. Shoham and M. Nehari, "Crime and Madness: Some Related Aspects of Breakdowns of Familial Interaction," *Int. Annals of Criminology,* Paris, 1971.

8. E. Bott, "Norms and Ideology: The Normal Family," Bell and Vogel, *Modern Introduction to the Family.* 450.

9. R. E. Maccoby, "Effects Upon Children of Their Mother's Outside Employment," Bell and Vogel, *Modern Introduction to the Family,* 521.

10. Maccoby, 499.

11. Maccoby, 510.

12. Thibaut and Kelley, 239.

13. A. F. Henry, "Family Role Structure and Self Blame," Bell and Vogel, 538.

14. S. Chillman, *Growing up Poor,* Washington, D. C.: Department of Health Education and Welfare, 1966.

15. J. Aronfreed, *Conduct and Conscience,* New York: Academic Press, 1963, 305.

16. Aronfreed, 203.

17. W. McCord, J. McCord and A. Howard, "Familial Correlates of Aggression in Nondelinquent Male Children," *J. Abn. & Soc. Psych,* 62 (1961), 79-83.

18. A. Bandura and R. W. Walters, *Adolescent Aggression,* New York: Ronald Press, 1950.

19. L. Kohlberg, "Development of Moral Character & Moral Ideology," in L. Hoffman and M. Hoffman (eds.), Review of Child Development Research. N. Y.: Russell Sage, 1964, 383-433.

20. Aronfreed, 316.

21. C. B. Ferster and J. B. Appel, "Punishment of S. Responding in Watching to Sample by Time-Out from Positive Reinforcement," *J. of Experimental Analysis of Behaviour,* 4 (1961), 45-56.

22. Aronfreed, 318.

23. E. H. Sutherland, *The Professional Thief,* Chicago, Ill.: University of Chicago Press, 1937.

24. E. W. Sutherland, *White Collar Crime,* New York: Dryden Press, 1949.

25. Sutherland, *White Collar Crime,* 97.

26. M. Grunhurt, "Statistics in Criminology," *J. Royal Stat. Soc.,* 114 (1951), 139-57.

27. U. S. Dept. of Justice, *Uniform Crime Report for the U. S. 1958,* Washington, D. C.: Federal Bureau of Investigation, 1959.

28. *The Challenge of Crime in a Free Society.* Report of the President's Commission on Law Enforcement and Administration of Justice, Washington, D. C. 1967.

29. S. E. Asch. *Social Psychology.* Englewood Cliffs, N. J.: Prentice Hall, 1952.

30. A. Bandura and R. H. Walters. *Social Learning and Personality Development.* New York: Holt, Rinehart & Winston, 1963.

References to Chapter III

1. R. K. Merton. *Social Theory and Social Structure.* New York: Free Press, 1957.

2. T. Freeman, J. L. Cameron, and MacGhie, *Chronic Schizophrenia.* London: Tavistock, 1958.

3. W. C. Reckless. "A Non-Causal Explanation: Containment Theory," *Excerpta Criminologica* (March/April, 1962), 131-34.

4. W. C. Reckless, S. Dinitz, and E. Murray. "Self-Concept as an Insulator Against Delinquency," *Am. Soc. Rev.,* 31 (1956), 744-46.

5. D. Glaser. "Criminality Theories and Behavioral Images," *Am. J. of Soc.,* 61 (1956) 433-44.

6. G. M. Sykes and D. Matza. "Techniques of Neutralization: A Theory of Delinquency," *Am. Soc. Rev.,* 22 (1951) 664-70.

7. D. R. Cressey. *Other People's Money.* New York: Free Press, 1953.

8. T. Parsons. *Essays in Sociological Theory.* New York: The Free Press, 1954, 304-05.

9. A. Cohen. *Delinquent Boys: The Culture of the Gang,* New York: Free Press, 1955.

10. E. M. Lemert. "An Isolation and Censure Theory of Naive Check Forgery," *J. Crim. Law, Criminology, and Police Science,* 44.

11. J. H. Gagnon and W. Simon, "Homosexuality: The Formulation of a Sociological Perspective," in M. Lefton, J. K. Skipper, and C. H. McCaghy (eds.), *Approaches to Deviance,* New York: Appleton-Century-Crofts, 1965.

12. A. J. Reiss. "The Social Integration of Queers and Peers," *Social Problems* 9 (1961), 102-20.

13. J. Genet. *The Thief's Journal.* New York: Grove Press, 1964, 21-167.

14. J. P. Sartre, *Saint-Genet, Comedian and Martyr.* New York: Braziller, Inc., 1952, 15.

15. J. Genet, *Thief's Journal,* 176.

16. B. Lewin. *L'Enfant Criminel.* Paris: Morihien Paul, 1949.

17. E. Durkheim. *Suicide: A Study in Sociology.* New York: Free Press, 1951, 250-53.

18. R. K. Merton, *Social Theory,* 131-60.

19. R. K. Merton. "Anomie, Anomia, and Social Interaction, Contexts of Deviant Behaviour," in M. B. Clinard (ed.), *Anomie and Deviant Behaviour,* New York: Free Press, 213.

20. L. Srole. "Social Integration and Certain Corollaries: An Exploratory Study," *Am. Soc. Rev.,* 21 (1956), 709-16.

21. M. Seeman. *"On the Meaning of Alienation,"* Am. Soc. Rev., 24 (1959), 789-91.

22. G. Lukac. *Existentialisme ou Marxisme?* Edition Nagel, Paris, 1948.

23. A. Camus. *The Myth of Sisyphus,* New York: Vintage Books, 1961, 23.

24. G. Lukacs. *On the Modes of Soul.* 1911.

25. D. Stafford-Clark. *Schizophrenia.* London: Pelican Books, 1951, 106.

26. R. W. White. *The Abnormal Personality.* New York: Ronald Press, 548.

27. Durkheim. *Suicide,* 81.

28. Merton. *Social Theory,* 153-54.

29. R. A. Cloward and L. B. Ohlin. *Delinquency and Opportunity.* New York: Free Press, 1961, 180-82.

30. R. R. Dynes, A. C. Clarke, and S. Dinitz. "Level of Aspirations: Some Aspects of Family Experience as a Variable," *Am. Soc. Rev.,* (1956), 212-14.

31. S. Shoman, N. Shapiro, and J. Spiegel. *The Vaga-bonds of Eilath.* Unpublished.

32. D. Riesman. *Individualism Reconsidered and Other Essays.* New York: Free Press, 1964.

33. A. Salomon. *The Tyranny of Progress.* New York: The Noonday Press, 1955.

34. Cohen. *Delinquent Boys.*

35. F. Tannenbaum. *Crime and the Community.* New York: Columbia University Press, 1938.

36. Cloward and Ohlin, *Delinquency and Opportunity,* 126.

37. J. C. Flugel. *Man, Morals and Society,* London: Pelican Books, 1955, 206-07.

38. W. G. Summer. *Folkways.* Boston: Ginn & Co., 1934, 27.

39. Aristotle. *Politics.*

40. J. Tenenbaum, *Race and Reich.* New York: Twayne, 1956, 11.

41. W. W. Buckland. *A Manual of Roman Private Law.* London: Cambridge University Press, 1939, 53.

42. Sumner, *Folkways,* 72.

43. H. S. Becker. *Outsiders: Studies in the Sociology of Deviance.* New York: Free Press, 1963.

44. E. Goffman. *Asylums.* New York: Anchor Books, 1961.

45. T. Mann. *The Holy Sinner.* London: Penguin Books, 1961, 197.

46. B. Bhattacharyya. *Guhyasamja-tantra,* 20, 98, 120.

47. Vital. *EtzHaim: Sha'ar Hakavanot.* Jerusalem: Mekor Haim, 1920, 47.

48. G. Scholem. *Major Trends in Jewish Mysticism.* New York: Schocken Books, 1941.

49. Scholem, *Jewish Mysticism,* 236.

50. S. Bichovsky. "A Psychiatric Evaluation of Frank and His Sect," *Hatkufa,* 15, (1932), 708.

51. S. Dubnow. *The History of the Jewish People.* Tel Aviv: Dvir, 1956, VII, 11.

52. C. G. Jung. *Evil.* Evanston, Ill.: Northwestern Univ. Press, 1967, 44.

53. Jung, *Evil,* 27.

54. Vital. *Sha'ar Hakelalim.*

55. C. G. Jung. *Aion.* London: Routledge, Kegan Paul, 1959, 44.

56. Jung, *Aion.*

57. Scholem, *Jewish Mysticism,* 308-09.

58. Bichovsky, "Frank and His Sect."

59. M. Eliade. *Yoga, Immortality and Freedom.* New York: Random House, 1969, 296-97.

60. Scholem, *Jewish Mysticism,* 237.

References to Chapter IV

1. E. M. Cioran. *The Temptation to Exist.* Chicago: Quadrangle Books, 1970.

2. D. Bell, "Crime as an American Way of Life," *The Antioch Review* (June, 1953) 13, 131-54.

3. T. D. Kemper. "Representative Roles and the Legitimation of Deviance," *Social Problems,* 13 (1966), 288-89.

4. Shlomo Shoham, Michal Ron-Menaker, Nura R'esh, and Salomon Rettig. *Value Systems in the Kibbutz Movement.* Unpublished research report, Institute of Criminology, Tel Aviv University, Israel.

5. S. Ranulf. *The Jealousy of the Gods and the Criminal Law in Athens.* Copenhagen: Levin and Munksgaard, 1933. Also, S. Ranulf. *Moral Indignation and Middle-Class Psychology: A Sociological Study.* Copenhagen: Levin & Munksgaard, 1933.

6. J. G. Frazer. *The Golden Bough.* London: MacMillan, 1960, 294.

7. E. E. Evans-Pritchard. *Witchcraft Oracles and Magic Among the Azande.* Oxford: The Clarendon Press, 1937, 114.

8. H. C. Lea. *A History of the Inquistion in the Middle Ages,* New York: Russel & Russel, 11, 110.

9. D. Krech, R. Crutchfield, and E. Ballachey. *The Individual in Society.* New York: McGraw Hill, 1962, 504.

10. Merton, *Social Theory,* 154.

11. Durkheim, *Suicide,* 156-61.

12. V. C. Wynne-Edwards. *Animal Dispersion in Relation to Social Behaviour,* London: Oliver & Boyd, 1962.

13. A. Artaut, *Les Temp Modernes,* February, 1949.

14. Durkheim, *Suicide.*

15. Merton, *Social Structure,* 134.

16. T. Sellin. *Culture Conflict and Crime.* New York: Social Science Research Council, 1938, 58.

17. Mannheim comments on the use of immigration as a medium of culture-conflict research: "The concept of culture-conflict covers a field much wider than the conflicts likely to arise through migration from one country to another with possibly very different language, mores and laws. In fact, however, it has been studied mainly in relation to the foreign immigrant where it provided a welcome ready-made opportunity to blame the immigrant for the increasing American crime rate." H. Mannheim. *Comparative Criminology.* London: Routledge & Kegan Paul, 1965, 539.

18. Sellin, *Culture Conflict & Crime,* Chapter IV. Also, T. Sellin. *The Conflict of Conduct Norms,* 57-107.

19. For additional studies, see: C. Van Vechten. "Criminality of the Foreign Born," *J. Crime and L. Criminology,* 32 (1941), 149-47; L. Savitz. "Delinquency and Migration," in M. E. Wolfgang, L. Savitz and N. Johnston, (eds.), *The Sociology of Crime and Delinquency.* New York: Wiley, 1970, 473-80; A. L. Wood. "Crime and Aggression in Changing Ceylon," *Transactions of the American Philosophical Society,* 51 (1961); *Immigrazione e Criminalita:*

Quaderni di Criminoliga Clinica, July-Sept., 1963, 347-58; S. Shoham. "The Application of the 'Culture-Conflict' Hypothesis to the Criminality of Immigrants in Israel," *J. Crime and L. Criminology,* (June, 1962), 207-17; and S. Shoham, N. Shoham, and A. Abd-El-Razek; "Immigration, Ethnicity and Ecology as Related to Juvenile Delinquency in Israel," *The British Journal of Criminology* (October, 1966), 391-409.

References to Chapter V

1. T. L. Wilkins. "The Concept of Cause in Criminology," *Issues in Criminology,* 3 (1968) 147-65.

2. A. K. Cohen. *Deviance and Control.* Englewood Cliffs, New Jersey: Prentice Hall, 1966, 88.

3. M. Eliade. *Immortality & Freedom.* New York: Random House, 272.

4. The Maggid of Mezritch. *Shemuah Tova.* Cited by R. Schatz-Oppenheimer, "Contemplative Prayer in Hassidism," *Studies in Mysticism and Religion.* (1967), 216.

5. P. Dudon. *Molinos.* Paris, 1921; also, *"Molinos," Dictionnaire de Theologique Catholique.*

6. S. Freud. *The Future of an Illusion.* New York: Doubleday, 1957, 3.

7. S. S. Angrist. "Mental Illness and Deviant Behaviour," *The Sociological Quarterly,* (1966).

8. A. R. Lindesmith & H. W. Dunham. "Some Principles of Criminal Typology," *Social Forces,* 19 (1941), 307-14.

9. M. B. Clinard. *Sociology of Deviant Behaviour.* 3d edition, 257.

10. D. R. Cressey. "The Criminal Tribes of India", *Sociology and Social Research,* 20 (1936) 503-11; 21 (1936), 18-25.

11. S. Shoham and M. Hovay. "Social Factors, Aspects of Treatment and Patterns of Criminal Career among the Bnei Tovim: A Study of Upper and Middle Class Juvenile Delinquency in Israel," *Human Relations,* 19 (1966), 1.

12. L. D. Jaffe. "Delinquency Proneness and Family Anomie," *Megamot,* 1962.

13. S. Shoham. "Conflict Situations and Delinquent Solutions," *Journal of Social Psychology,* 69 (1964), 82-215.

14. T. Parsons. *Essays in Sociological Theory.* New York: The Free Press, 1954, 304-05.

15. A. K. Cohen. *Delinquent Boys: The Culture of the Gang.* New York: Free Press, 1955.

16. E. H. Erikson. "The Problem of Identity, *"Journal of American Psychiatric Association,* IV (1956).

17. E. G. Schachtel. *Metamorphosis.* London: Routledge, Kegan Paul, 1963.

18. G. Sykes & D. Matza. "Techniques of Neutralization, A Theory of Delinquency," *American Sociological Review,* 22 (1957), 664-70.

19. J. Galbraith. *The Affluent Society.* London: H. Hamilton, 1960.

20. D. Reisman. *The Lonely Crowd.* New Haven: Yale University Press, 1961.

21. T. R. Fyvel. *The Insecure Offenders.* London: Chatto and Windus, 1961.

22. S. Shoham. "Conflict Situations and Delinquent Solutions."

23. C. R. Shaw and H. D. MacKay. *Juvenile Delinquency and Urban Areas.* Chicago: University of Chicago Press, 1942.

24. T. Morris. *The Criminal Area.* London: Routledge, Kegan Paul, 1958.

25. D. Christiansen. "Industrialization and Urbanization in Relation to Crime and Juvenile Delinquency," *International Rev. of Criminal Policy,* 1960.

26. Shoham and Hovav. "Social Factors."

27. W. A. Bonger. *Criminality and Economic Condition.* Boston: Little Brown, 1916.

28. E. Ferri. *Criminal Sociology.* Boston: Little Brown, 1900. Also, M. Ploscowe. "Some Causative Factors in Criminality: Report on the Causes of Crime," *Report of the National Commission on Law.* Government Printing Office, 1931, 114-16.

29. A. K. Cohen. *Delinquent Boys: The Culture of the Gang.* New York: Free Press, 1955.

30. G. Von Mayr. *Statistik der Gesichtlichen Polizei un Konigreiche Bayern und in einigen anderen Landern.* Munich, 1867.

31. T. Sellin. *Research Memorandum on Crime in the Depression.* New York: Social Science Research Council, 1937.

32. S. Degrazia. *The Political Community, A Study of Anomie.* Chicago: 1948, 71.

33. D. Glaser, "Criminal Theories and Behavioural Images," *Amer. J. Sociol.,* 61, 435-44.

34. W. B. Miller. *Delinquent Behaviour, Culture and the Individual.* Washington, D. C.: National Education Association, 1959, 74-75.

35. R. A. Cloward and L. E. Ohlin. *Delinquency and Opportunity, A Theory of Delinquent Gangs.* New York: The Free Press, 1960.

36. D. R. Cressey. "Role Theory and Compulsive Crimes," in D. R. Cressey and D. A. Ward (eds.), *Delinquency, Crime and the Social Process.* New York: Harper and Row, 1969. 1124-128.

37. Cressey and Ward, *Delinquency,* 503.

38. W. A. Rushing, *Deviant Behaviour and Social Process.* Chicago: Rand, McNally, 1969, 328.

39. M. E. Wolfgang. *Studies in Homicide.* New York: Harper and.Row, 1967, 75.

40. E. H. Sutherland and D. R. Cressey. *Principles of*

Criminology. Philadelphia: Lippincott, 1967, 80.

41. A. K. Cohen. *Delinquent Boys.*

42. W. F. Whyte. *Street Corner Society,* Chicago: Univ. Press, 1943.

43. W. B. Miller. "Lower Class Culture as a Generating Milieu of Gang Delinquency," *Journal of Social Issues,* 14 (1958), 9.

44. Cloward and Ohlin. *Delinquency and Opportunity.*

45. F. M. Thrasher. *The Gang.* Chicago: Chicago Univ. Press, 1927.

46. H. Bloch and A. Niederhoffer, *The Gang, A Study in Adolescent Behaviour,* New York: Philosophical Library, 1958.

47. E. Erikson. "The Problem of Identity," *Journal of American Psychiatric Association,* IV (1956).48. R. K. Merton. *Social Theory and Social Structure.* New York: Free Press, 1957.

49. F. Tannenbaum. *Crime and the Community.* New York: Columbia University Press, 1938.

50. H. W. Zorbaugh. *The Gold Coast and the Slum.* Chicago: Chicago Univ. Press, 1929.

51. W. C. Kvaraceus. *Dynamics of Delinquency.* Columbus, Ohio: Charles E. Merrill, 1966.

52. D. Matza. *Delinquency & Drift,* New York: Wiley, 1964.

53. Miller, "Lower Class Culture," 68.

54. R. K. Merton. *Social Theory,* 225.

55. Kvaraceus, *Dynamics,* 4.

56. M. Sherif and H. Contril. *The Psychology of Ego Involvement.*

57. Matza, *Delinquency,* 52.

References to Chapter VI

1. L. A. Coser. The Functions of Social Conflict. New York: Free Press, 1956, 151-56.

2. B. Russell. *A History of Western Philosophy,* London: Allen and Unwin, 1947, 62-63.

3. S. Freud. Collected Papers, Vol. 2. London: Hogarth Press, 1924, 107.

4. W. K. Kaufmann. *Critique of Religion and Philosophy.* New York: Anchor Books, 1961, 420-21.

5. W. R. Lange. *The Philosophy of Plotinus.* London: Green and Co., 62.

6. L. A. Coser. "Some Functions of Deviant Behaviour and Normative Flexibility," *Journal of Sociology,* 69 (1962), 172-81.

7. "Minutes of Evidence," *Royal Commission on Capital Punishment,* 1949-1953, 207.

8. F. Alexander and H. Staub. *The Criminal, the Judge and the Public.* New York: Free Press, 1957, 215.

9. H. Weihofen. *The Urge to Punish.* Bloomington: Indiana University Press, 1956, 28.

10. L. A. Coser. *The Function of Social Conflict,* 785.

11. A. K. Daniels and R. R. Daniels. "The Social Function of the Career Fool," *Psychiatry,* 27 (August, 1964), 219-29.

12. A. K. Cohen. *Deviance and Control,* 10.

13. J. G. Frazer, *The Golden Bough,* 753.

14. H. Brunner. *Grundzuge der Deutschen Rechtsgeschichte.* Leipzig, 1901, 68.

15. J. Steinbeck. *Travels With Charley.* New York: Bantam Books, 143.

16. C. Wirszubski. *The Shabbatean Ideology of the Apostasy of the Messiah,* 1938, 224.

17. S. Shoham. *The Mark of Cain,* New York: Oceana Publications, 1970.

Index